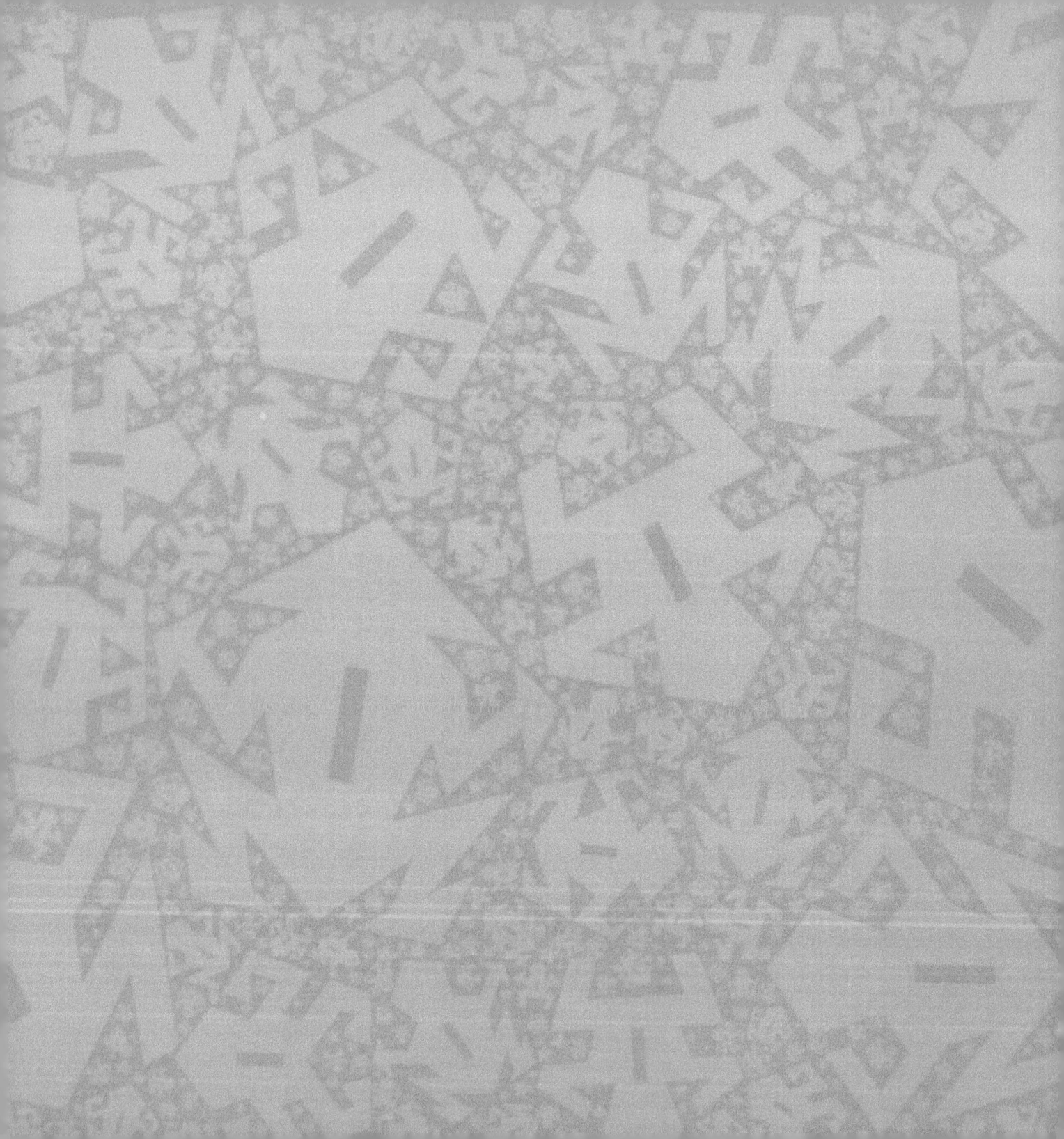

IMAGE & WORD: *A Dialectic*

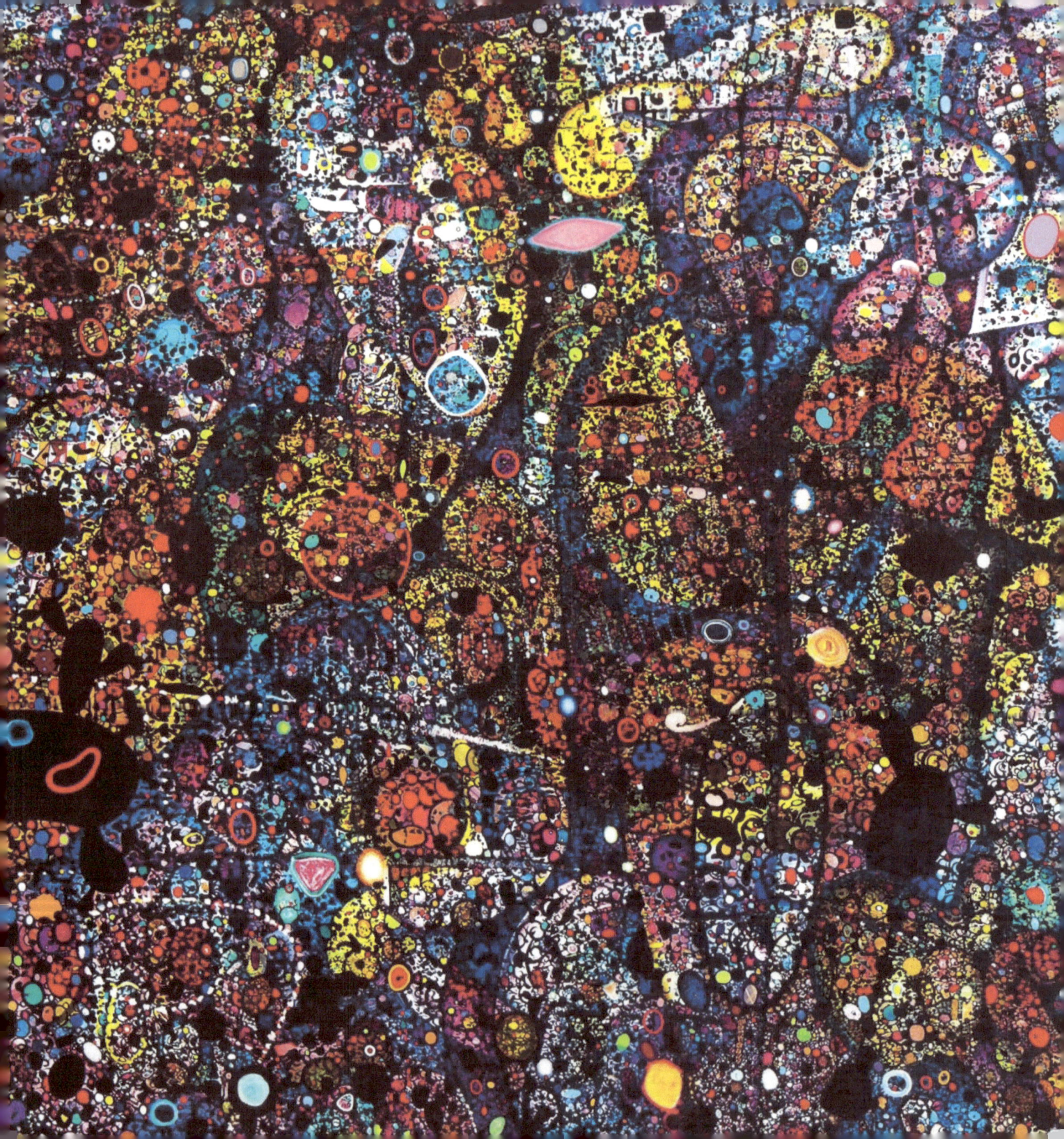

IMAGE & WORD: *A Dialectic*

Bonnie Bostrom   responds to   Vytas Sakalas

Foreword by Patricia Hills

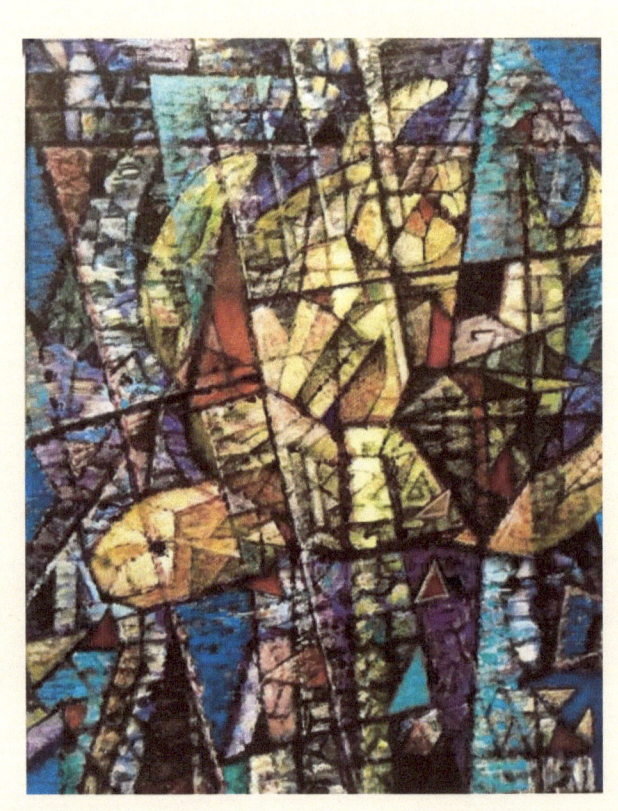

*To Torin Thomas Bostrom
and the wonderful future
he brings to our family.*

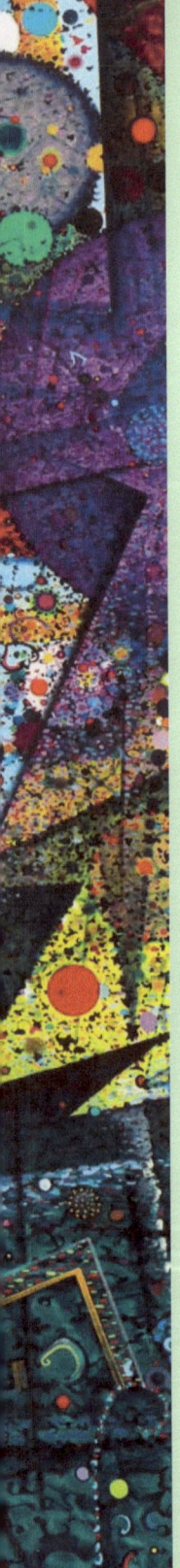

TABLE OF CONTENTS

FOREWORD: Remembering Vytas

"When I'm painting, I feel that I'm participating in the ongoing creation of the universe."

Vytas Sakalas

I first met Vytas Sakalas in 1975, in the second year that I was teaching art history courses at York College, one of the City University of New York four-year colleges. At that time York had a student body comprised largely of second-generation immigrants and working class students who had to support themselves. As a transfer student from Los Angeles City College and a studio major, he would have taken required art history courses, including my courses focused on the modern period. I noticed him immediately in the classroom as the tall, blond Lithuanian American youth, who went by the name of Vytautas Sakalauskas.

Verbally astute, if somewhat dreamy, he was dedicated to his ideals and determination to think like an artist and live like an artist. It was a pleasure to have him in the classroom, making observations about art that challenged textbook platitudes; moreover, his dedication to independent thinking served as an encouragement to the other students. Without a doubt he was the smartest, most competent, and most intellectual student I had in my four years of teaching some 800 students at York College.

He was also generously helpful. When there were cutbacks by the city, and class sizes began to triple, he helped by handling equipment and monitoring the large jumbo classes I was teaching. By the time he graduated he had become friends with my family, who even today remember him fondly.

At York College he began his cloud paintings. He was taking a painting course from the chair of the department, Arthur Anderson, whose assignment to the students was to pick and develop a theme generated by things in the natural world. Vytas, already committed to drawing from his own imagination for his paintings' subjects, chose clouds to paint. Although respectful of his teachers, including Ernest Garthwaite who encouraged his abstract painting and Elena Borstein who taught him photography, he stubbornly resisted their tampering with his inner vision. He produced many canvases of white and grey clouds against a graded blue background. They were like Rococo ceiling paintings without allegorical figures and putti, wherein the clouds themselves thrust and parry often with half menacing intentions. Above all, they were not serene but contained energies to sweep the viewer up into an expanding universe. It is no wonder that in 2000 he returned to the cloud theme, an imagery continuously conducive to further meanderings of the mind.

In 1978 I moved with my family to Boston to teach at Boston University. Vytas had also moved there with his wife Gražina. He was invited to participate in a group exhibition, Illusion in Art: Perception/Description/Deception, held in 1987 at the Boston University Art Gallery, which I then directed. He included three of his cutouts, one of which was installed high on the wall. The effect was like seeing through windows into another universe.

In 1989 Vytas moved to Sedona, Arizona. To me it was fitting, as it was the place where the surrealist artist Max Ernst had moved during the 1940s. The desert, the cactus, the rock formations, and surrealism, fit Vytas's artistic temperament. Some of the works, such as Cow Skull with Cacti (1993-94) and Boots and Hat by Window (1995) seem to have been inspired by the early-20th century American expressive cubists who lived in the Southwest. Generally, his paintings of the late 1990s and first decade of the 21st century became filled with geometric and/or biomorphic detail not connected to the world of specific objects. Filled with energy they simultaneously project a mystical quality.

We continued to be in touch. He visited Boston to introduce us to his son, Darius, whom he was raising as a single parent. After he moved to Tucson, the artist May Stevens and I visited him in 2000 at the time of Rudolf Baranik's memorial exhibition at the University of Arizona Museum of Art. (Baranik was also a Lithuanian who had been married to Stevens, and he knew Vytas). We were impressed by Vytas's prodigious output of magnificent paintings – paintings inspired by organic shapes, mineral formations, plant textures, astronomical forms, even neon lights – the macro and micro universe - as well as mathematical and fractal forms.

The genius of Vytas is that he has always

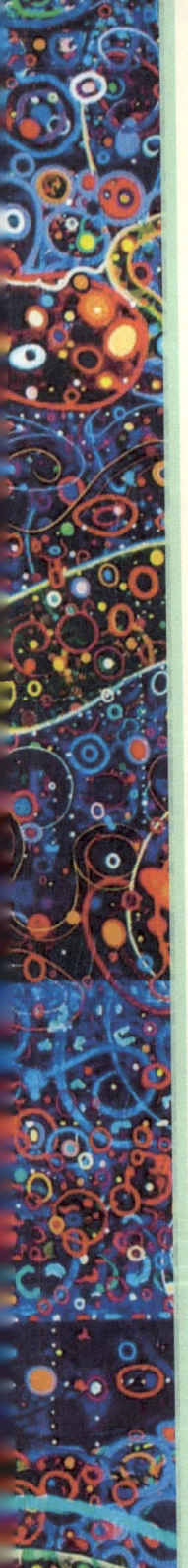

been able to alternate canvases with ease; painting a canvas of minimalist abstraction and then switching to a canvas filled with textured, dense non-objective elements. Some of his early abstract paintings are devoid of overt detail, such as Anticipating Fulfillment (1969). Other early paintings capture a deep surrealist space, such as Kwhepsahnt (1971). Intricate forms of colored shapes and lines dance about in works such as Bell Rock, Sedona (1998-2008) and Planets (2005-2010). These paintings were followed by large paintings of gentle biomorphic shapes, such as Atmansphere 17 (2004-2016), or the kinetic pulsing and otherworldly colors of Golden Light (2006-2016).

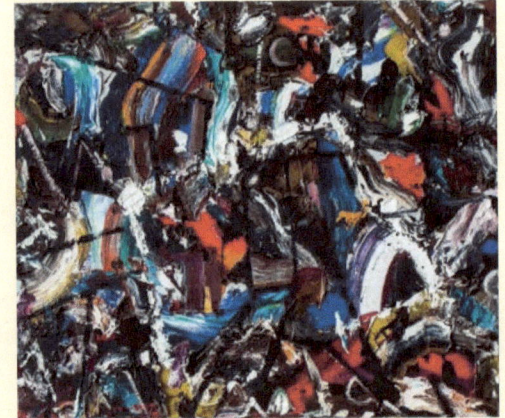

These complex compositions draw in the viewer who loses her or his quotidian consciousness in Vytas' "trance-formations". That is what Vytas offers his viewers: the promise of another universe, a parallel universe of pure sensation.

Patricia Hills, PhD
Professor Emerita
Dept. of History of Art & Architecture
Boston University, Boston, MA

ARTIST'S STATEMENT

The seemingly magical process of creation, of somehow making something out of nothing, I find endlessly fascinating; a need at the core of my being. While nature is my greatest inspiration, an underlying premise of my work is that valuable knowing and understanding of the nature of reality can be gained by going inward and manifesting outwardly through art.

My creative process usually begins with simply looking at a surface, be it paper, canvas, metal, etc., and responding to it. As I stare at the 'blank' surface, gradually shapes, dots, lines, colors begin to appear to me, like subtle hallucinations, and I draw or paint them in. Many, especially the larger structures, are felt viscerally as well as seen. It is often something in the surface texture of the material I'm using that suggests what I see, so the visions and hallucinations that develop are inextricably bound up with the physical media I'm employing. In this process I soon enter a mild state of trance in which I'm being led ever deeper into the unknown.

By remaining open to whatever may appear, I end up discovering things that I had never seen before. This often involves a great deal of change as the work develops, and by the time it is completed it has usually been completely transformed ('tranceformed'). I consider the work 'complete' when it has become fully alive in an autonomous way and there is no more to be 'seen' in it (or new things no longer

appear). Some works achieve only a provisional completeness and could be worked on (theoretically) for the rest of my life. Many of my works have taken years to reach a state of completeness.

I find that I tend to enjoy working at or near the ends of the minimal to maximal spectrum. I always had great respect and admiration for the masters of Sumi-e painting, as well as for the Pointillists. Indeed, I admire all the great artists of history, but especially Cezanne, Van Gogh, Picasso, Matisse, Mondrian, and Čiurlionis. Although Čiurlionis is not as well known as the others, he is regarded by many as being Lithuania's greatest artistic hero. Some art historians, (including non-Lithuanians) familiar with his work consider him to be the first artist to paint abstractly, though most of his work is closer to Symbolism in style.

The exploration of the psychological realm by the Surrealists, Abstract Expressionists, and others has provided inspiration for my work which I call Tranceformationism.

I believe this visionary process can open up a whole new way of perceiving and being, and even act as a healthy alternative to drugs, alcohol, and some mass media as a means of inducing trance. I sincerely hope, dear viewer, that this particular collection of visions that I have chosen from my body of work will have a good effect on you.

Vytas Sakalas

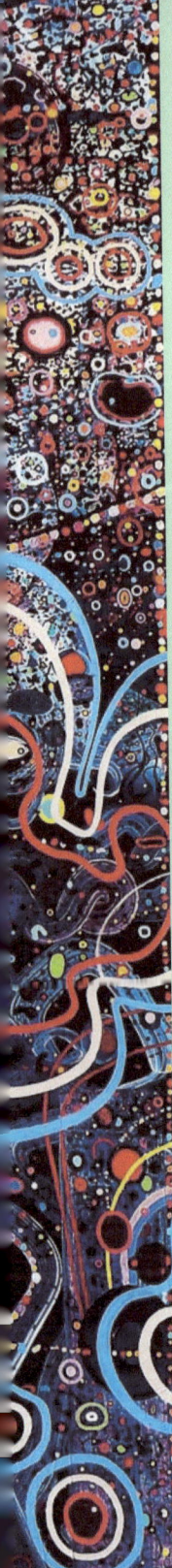

INTRODUCTION

The most challenging part of writing this book was coming up with the title. I wanted something that would convey what the book attempts to accomplish and at the same time did not want to be misleading. At first it was to be called a synthesis, then dialogue, and finally, I chose the word dialectic. All the images are created by Vytas and the interpretations of those visions are all mine. The dialectic is between his images and the prose poems I have written after witnessing his work. I spent wonderful times in his studio; totally captivated by the many paintings he had completed and watching his works in progress.

Dialectic has many meanings but what I intend with this book is captured beautifully in a paper written by Kim O'Connor at the University of Chicago. In writing on Theories of Media (2003), Kim explains that…."dialectic can be a useful way to conceptualize subject/object relationships in any number of contexts, particularly artistic contexts. Dialectic allows us to break down the bifurcated model of spectator/artwork so that, for example, it becomes possible for both the reader and writer to create meaning in a poem, and for an abstract painting to reveal something intrinsic to both artwork and beholder." So the creation of a painting is done initially in the mind of the artist and comes to fruition in the mind of the viewer; dialectic.

The easiest part of this project was responding to the artwork of Vytas Sakalas. When I first visited his studio I thought I would fall to my knees. I am not given to hyperbole so when I say "to my knees," I felt what the poet Greg Hart refers to as "reverence" for Vytas' paintings. As a writer, I am constantly engaging with information so I can translate what arises in my mind into something external. It is an addictive process. I see images, either visually or "imaginally" and writing is my way of encapsulating those images into word code for the reader to unlock.

I hope I have not intruded but have presented my interpretation in such a way that you have an opportunity to experience a magical event creating another level of dialectic; your response to our images and words. I am not presenting a learned critique or an exercise in critical theory. I am trying to take you hostage for a moment so you can witness, with me, the extraordinary work of a modern genius, Vytas Sakalas.

Bonnie Bostrom

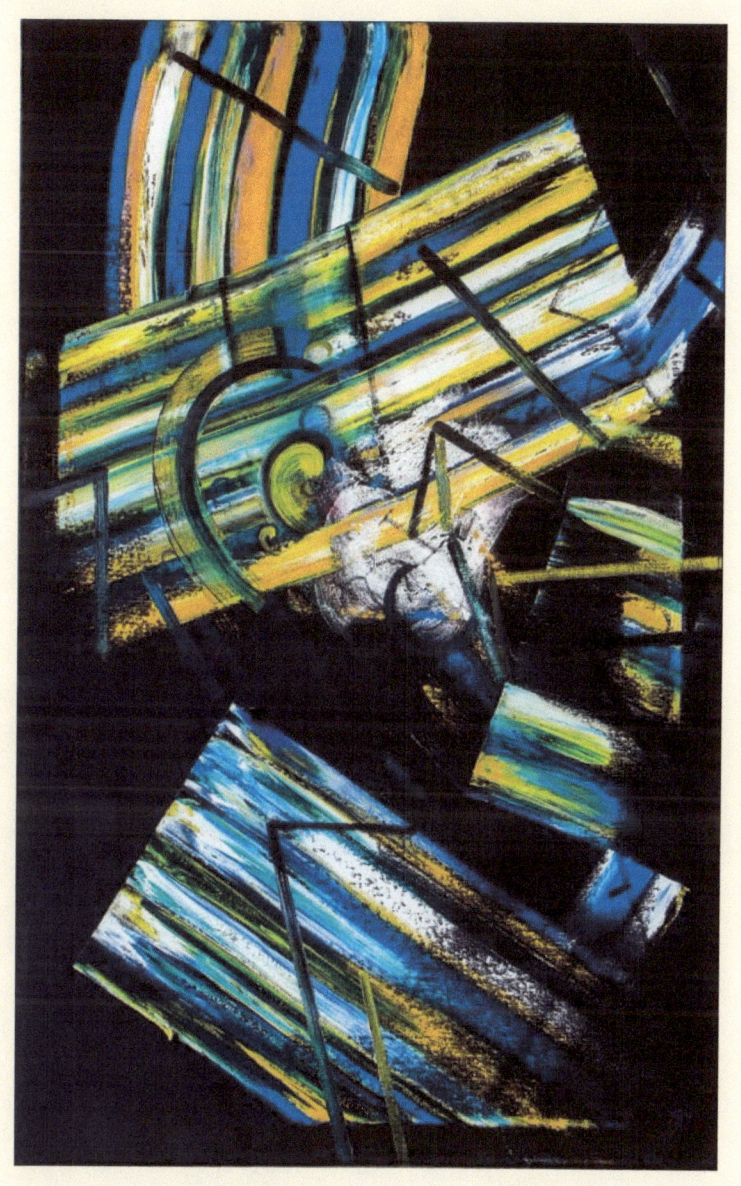

THE ONENESS

1970 - 1971
Oil on Canvas
48" x 48"

This, one of the earliest pieces we have of Vytas' work, is riveting. At eighteen he shows the perspicacity and prophecy of emerging genius. The central image, though not recognizable as something we can name, is familiar. Fallopian tubes, the sun as ovum, the emergence of life on a forming planet; all a meta-narrative of the story his life will play out as an artist. In the images to follow, we will see elements of this fledgling work and be amazed at the flight his mind affords.

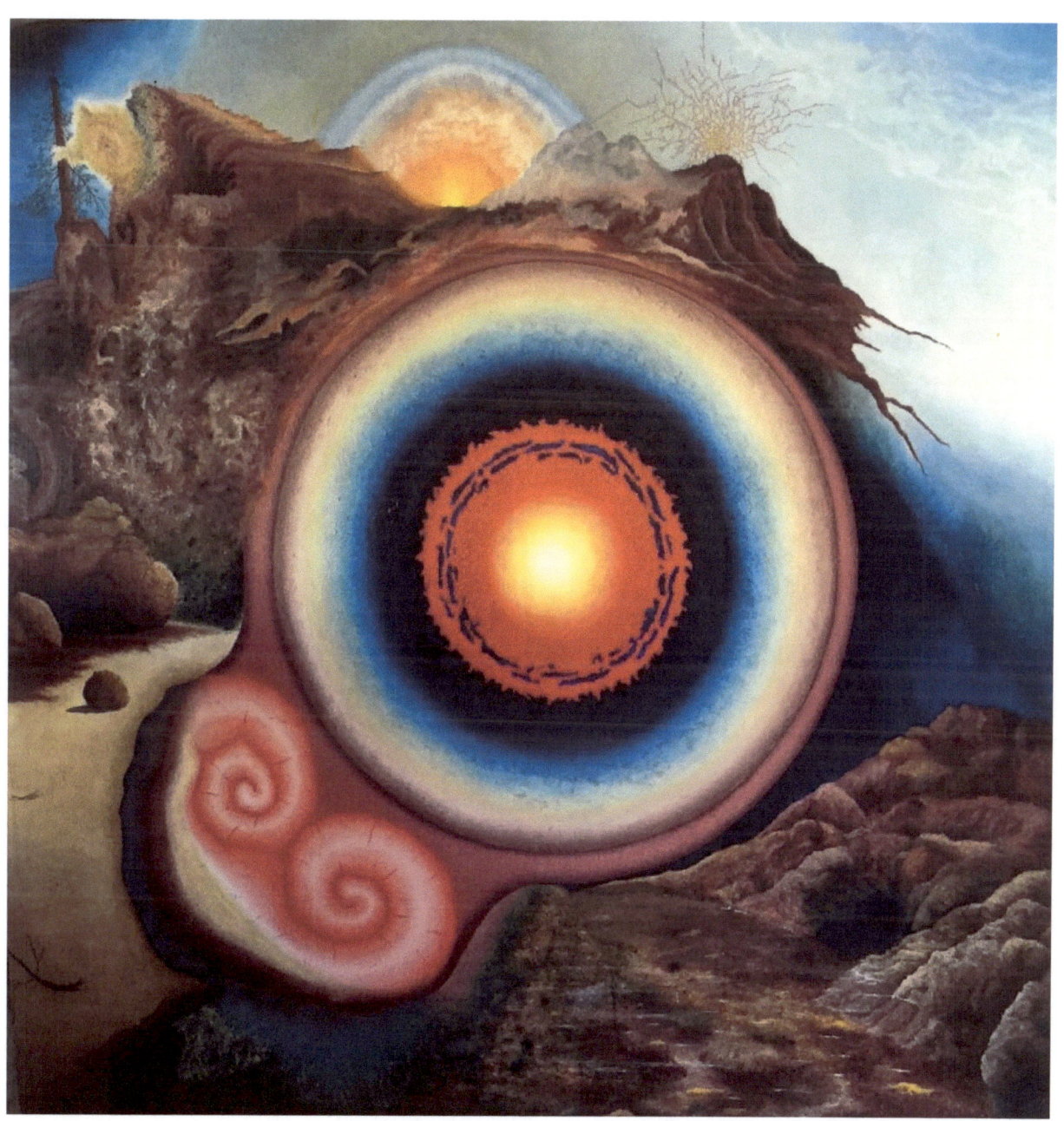

ANTICIPATING FULFILLMENT

1969
Oil on Canvas
30" x 24"

Wow. It is not difficult to apprehend blatant sexual references in this rather startling work. Visual metaphors evoke the deep structure of interplay between image and thought. The glans blossom of youthful virility, the vaginal door, the erect stem; all suggesting the meta narrative of what is probably symbolic of an early love affair. It is a lovely homage to the drive that propels us all toward creative and procreative acts.

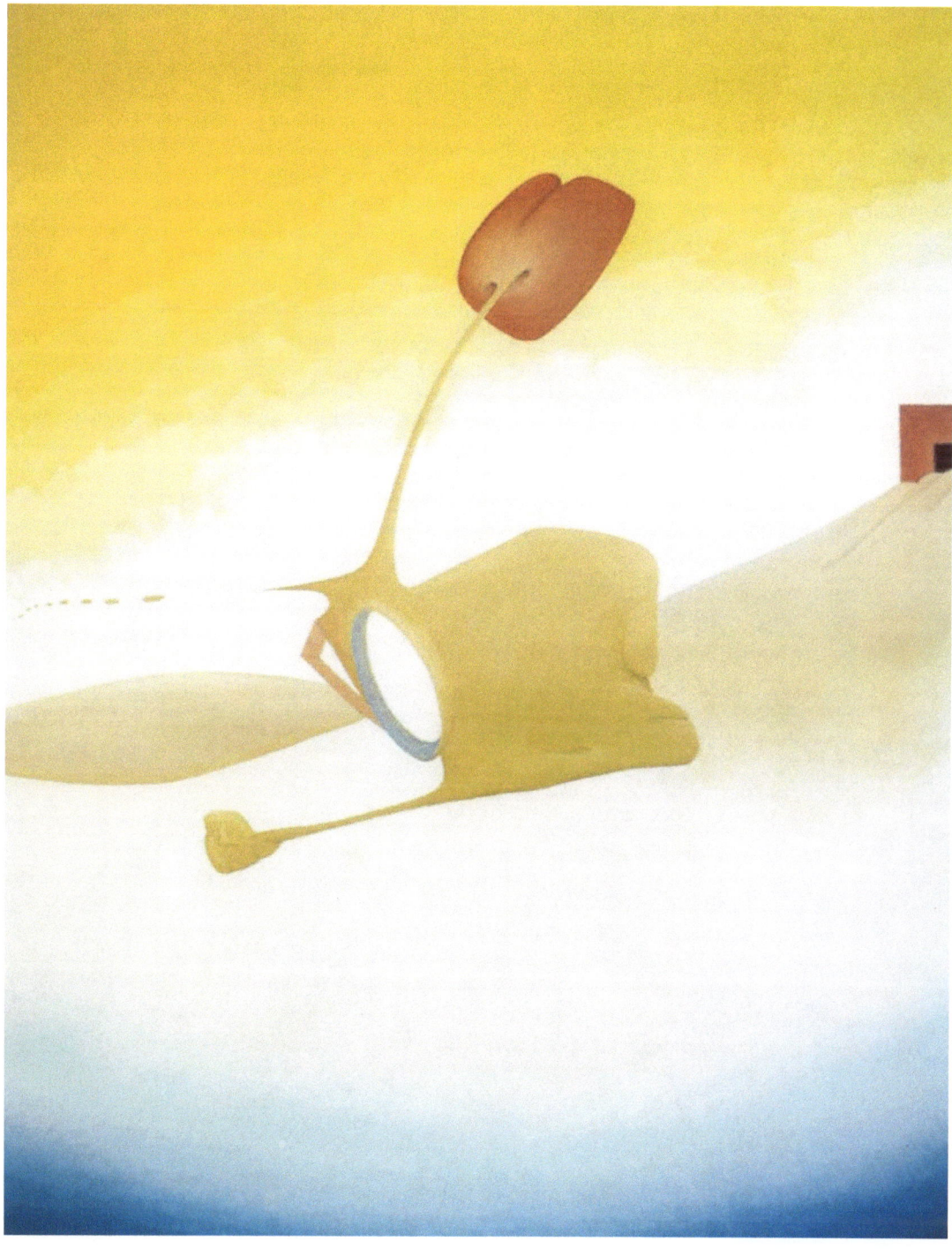

THE NOUMENON

1971
Oil on Canvas Board
30" x 24"
Stolen from New York City Studio in 1974

From Teilhard de Chardin's noosphere to Kantian noumenon, Vytas was aware of transcendental aesthetic and logic. In his late teens and early twenties, he was grappling with notions of whether a guessed at "noumenal" world could be apprehended by the senses or merely inferred. Beyond that, he was attempting to represent this "thing in itself" visually; quite an undertaking for a nineteen year old artist. He addresses the canvas heroically and fruitfully. There are, in this world of Vytas, many elements that will later receive the benefit of his early explorations into the transcendental analytic.

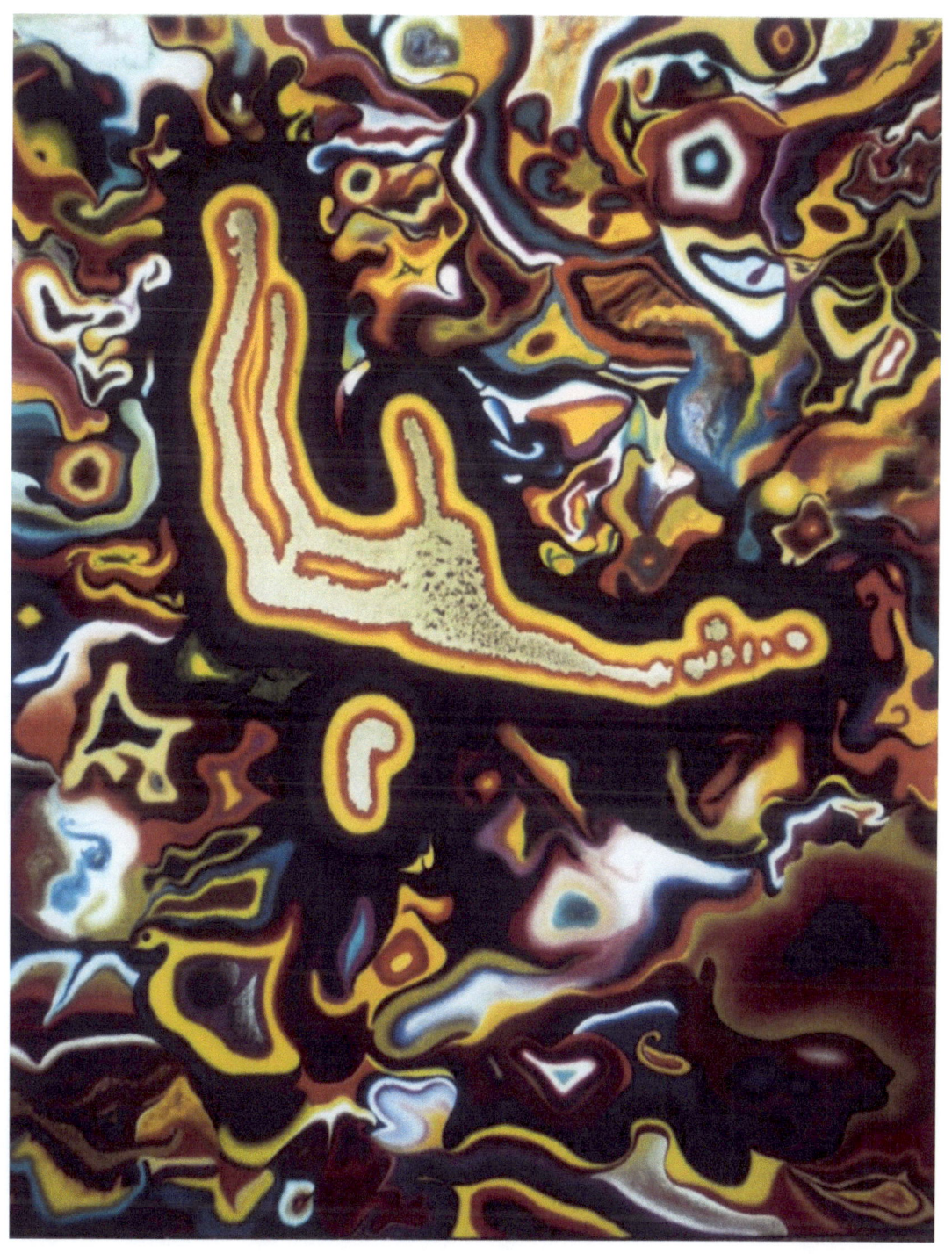

KWHEPSAHNT

1971
Oil and Spray Enamel on Canvas
18" x 24"
Collection of National Čiurlionis Art Museum
Kaunas, Lithuania

What fascinates in this piece is how he uses light. The organic looking object with the red "eye" is self radiant, and touched by a light source, simultaneously. There are shadowy places, places illuminated and, in the lower part of the painting, a riot of color and action takes a prominent place. During this time period the Surrealists would have been a major influence. This work calls to mind the work of Tanguy and his wife, Kay Sage, as well as that of Dali, Miro and Ernst. Their works are called to mind, yes, but Vytas moves beyond their influence into his own strangely compelling territory.

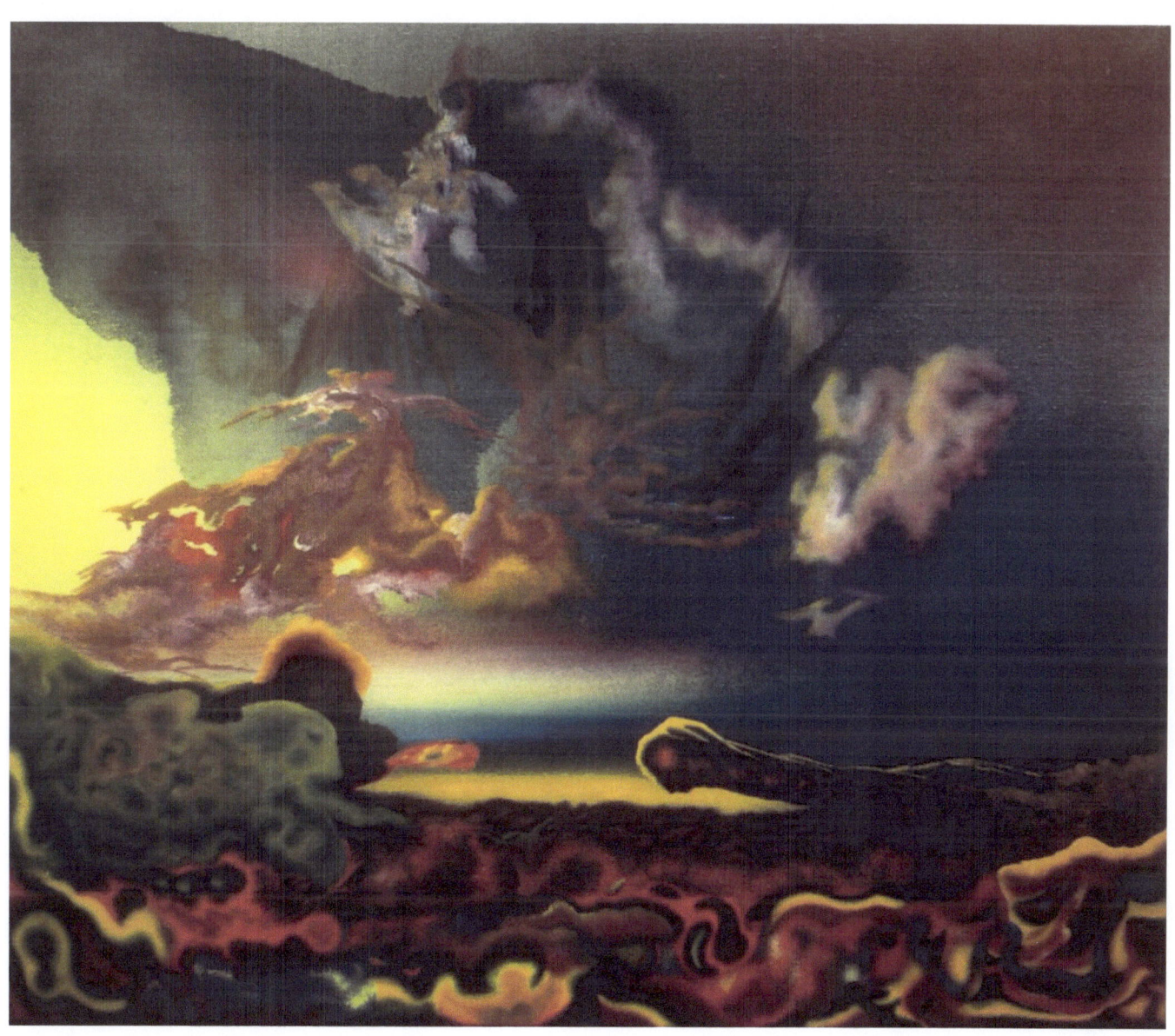

THE DEHISCENCE

1972
Oil on Canvas
40" x 36"
Stolen from New York City Studio in 1974

Explosive dehiscence is a ballistic mechanism of plants whereby they disperse seeds outward as far as 100 feet. The process involves splitting and may result in parts of the plant being completely separated. In addition to plant behavior, this piece brings to mind Stanislav Grof's theories of human birth and the trauma of separation from the womb. Vytas has provided a meta-narrative of birthing. Vestigial animal forms, an exploding womb, partially formed homunculi; all contained under a blue sky and grounded in what appears to be earth, tell the story.

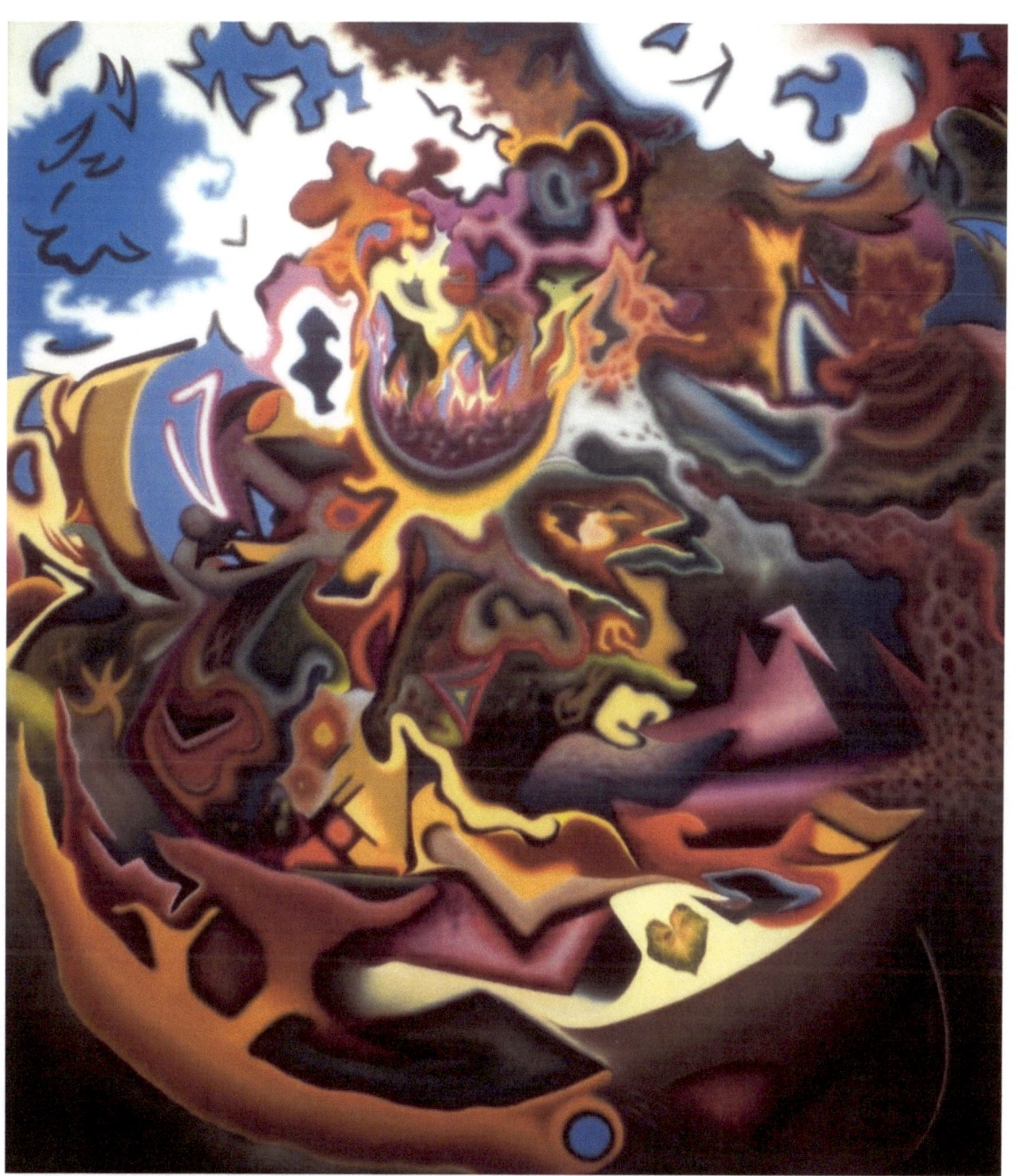

NATURE'S PATTERN 2

1974
Oil on Canvas
24" x 30"
Stolen from New York City Studio in 1974

Vytas explores connections in 2D that make it seem like we are inside a living structure. Dendritic forms, neuronal activity, leaf meal magnified, cellular architecture; the deep designs of life. Much of Vytas' early work elevates organic interstitial patterns. As his career progresses, the organic will be magnified, sometimes shattered by geometric abstraction, but will remain a consistent motif in his work.

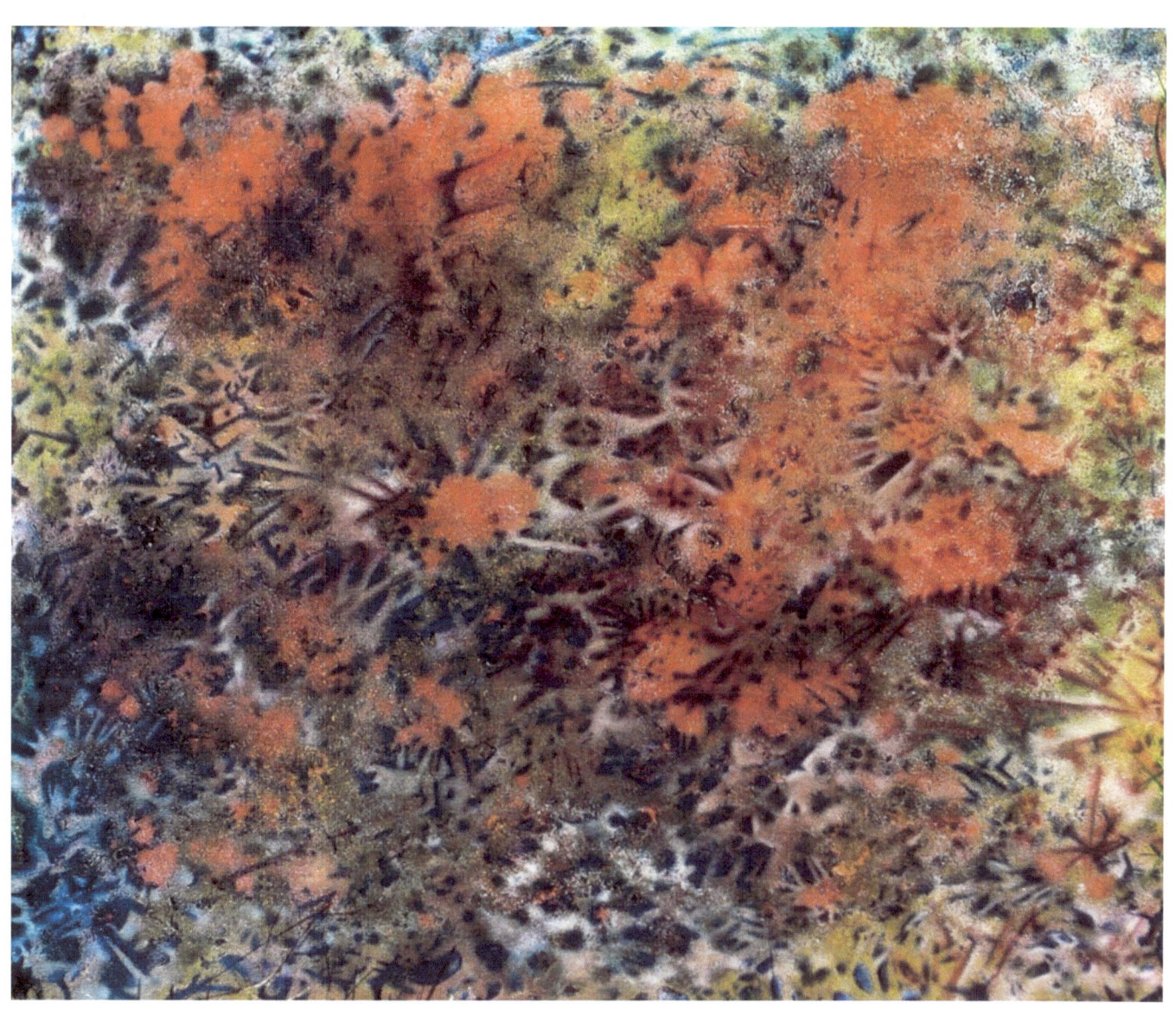

FLESH SPACE

1975
Acrylic on Canvas Board
39" x 29"

Another of his early works; this is a map of secret places. A magical, biological, path leads us into the heart of an atom or into the smallest imaginable cell of life. The curvilinear forms define a trajectory we follow, finding our way deep into this organic territory. Viewed from within, his construction binds our imagination to symbolic representations of sexuality. We might think of this as the sacred nature of skin.

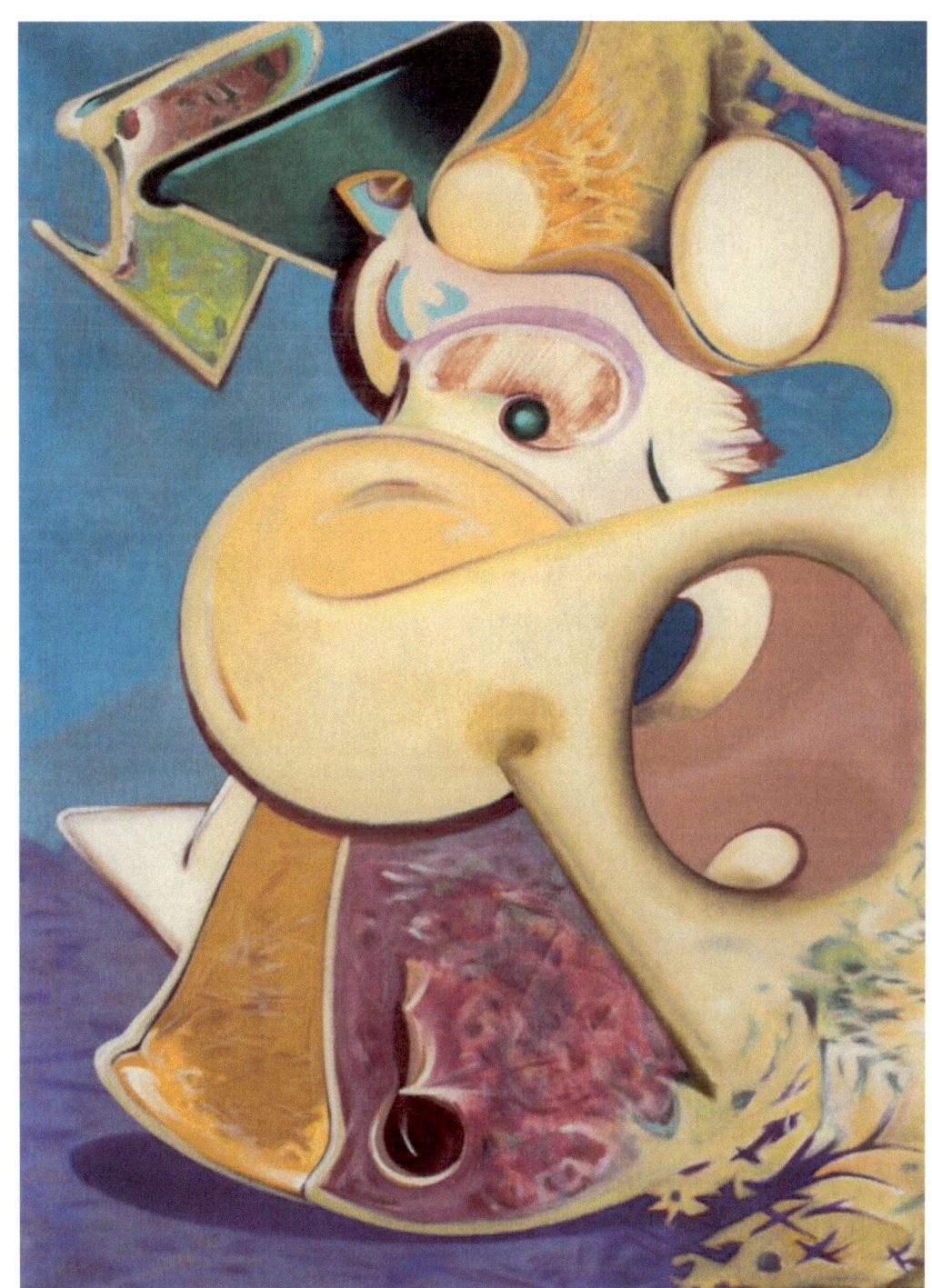

CLOUD SONATA

1975 - 1976
Acrylic on Canvas
54" x 40"

This early painting reminds me of the Buddhist expression Sky-like Mind. It speaks to the impermanence of thought. Each cloud is an obscuration of the clarity of pure awareness. The darker corner on the lower right side suggests the unconscious and all the darkness that waits to come into the light of consciousness. It seems Vytas's quest is to make a cohesive whole.

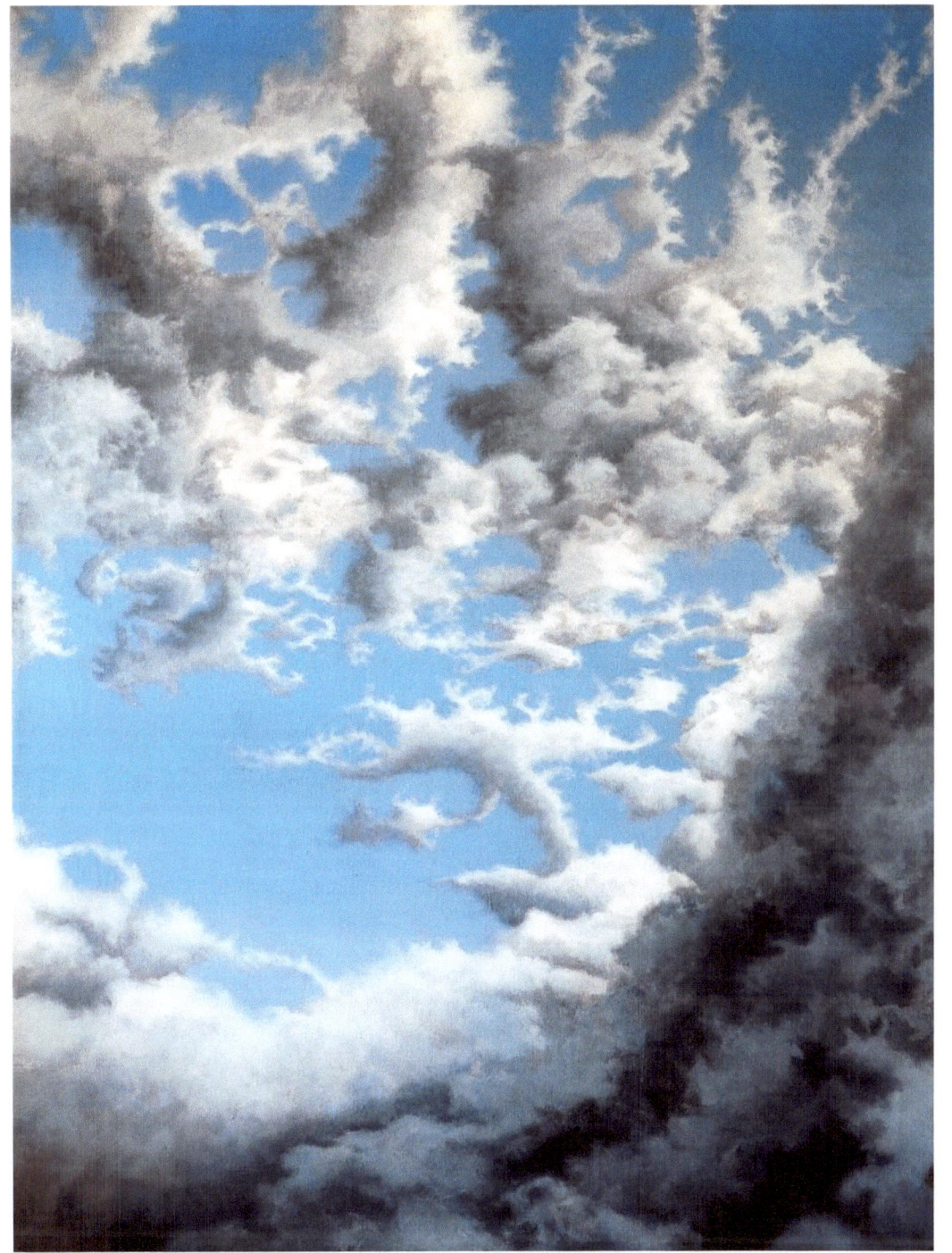

CLOUD INTERNALIZATION

1976 - 1981
Oil on Canvas
20" x 22"
Collection of National Čiurlionis Art Museum
Kaunas, Lithuania

The series of cloud paintings shows tremendous versatility in viewpoint, treatment and palette. Clouds have been of significant interest for Vytas. Here we are drawn into soft forms and tender color. In the background, discernable outlines of full clouds play with the crystal geometrics of rainwater. All rain begins as snow and even a medium sized cloud weighs several ton. Vytas has an unprecedented understanding of the organic quality of the atmosphere. We begin to understand that clouds are alive. They bear water; the source of all that has come into being as life.

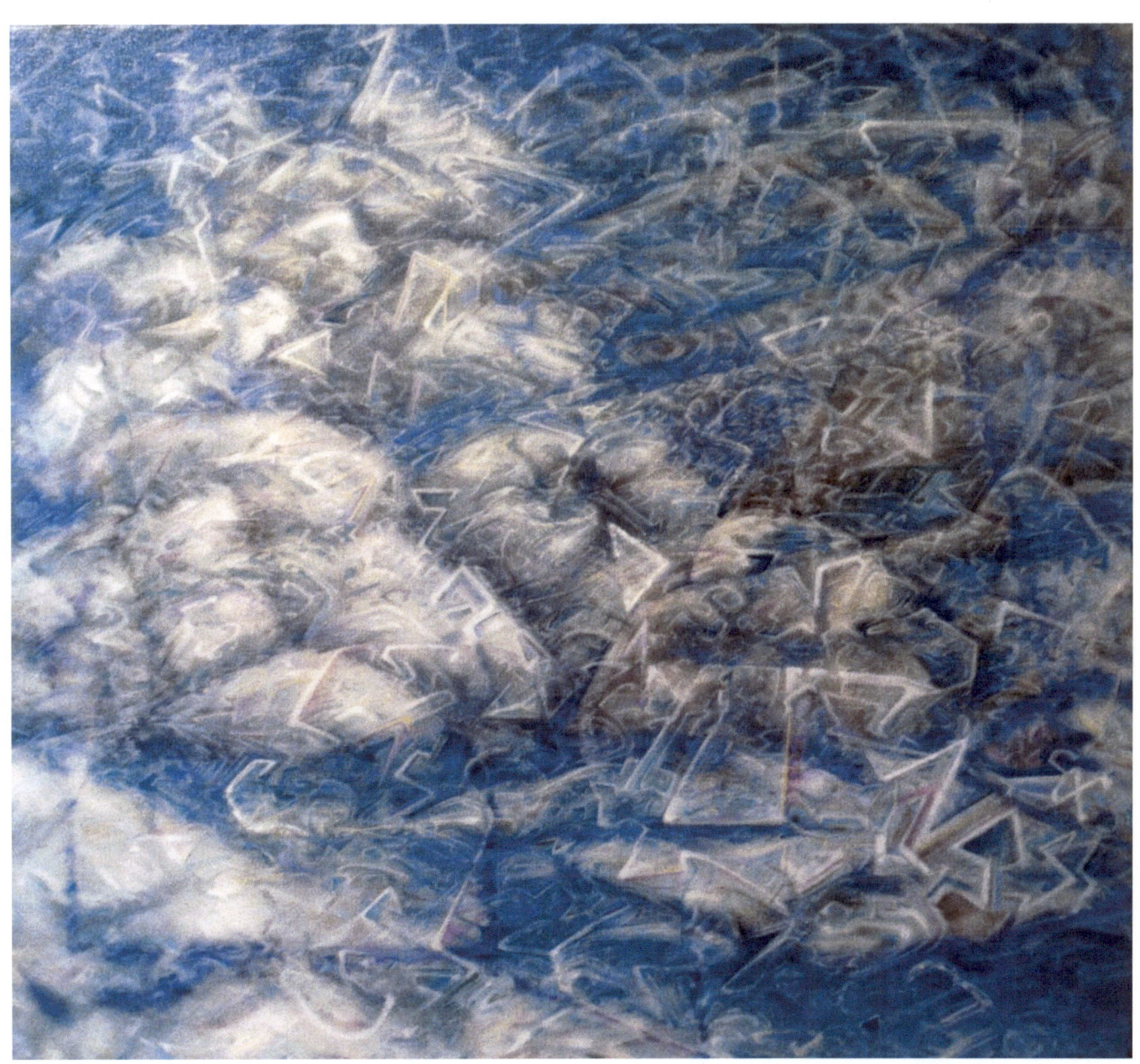

ON THE TABLE (STONE CLOUDS)

1978
Mixed Media on Mat Board
17" x 14"
Collection of National Čiurlionis Art Museum
Kaunas, Lithuania.

Massive mechanics of motion, caught in the freeze frame of Vytas' eye, lures us into this environment. Deeply archetypal, these forms remind us of the chalk stone of old bones and negative space defines ancient mystery. Rock is turning to jewel as it tumbles soundless in the dark. Time, invisible, leaves its deadly trace on every element in this work except for the golden arrows leading us up and out.

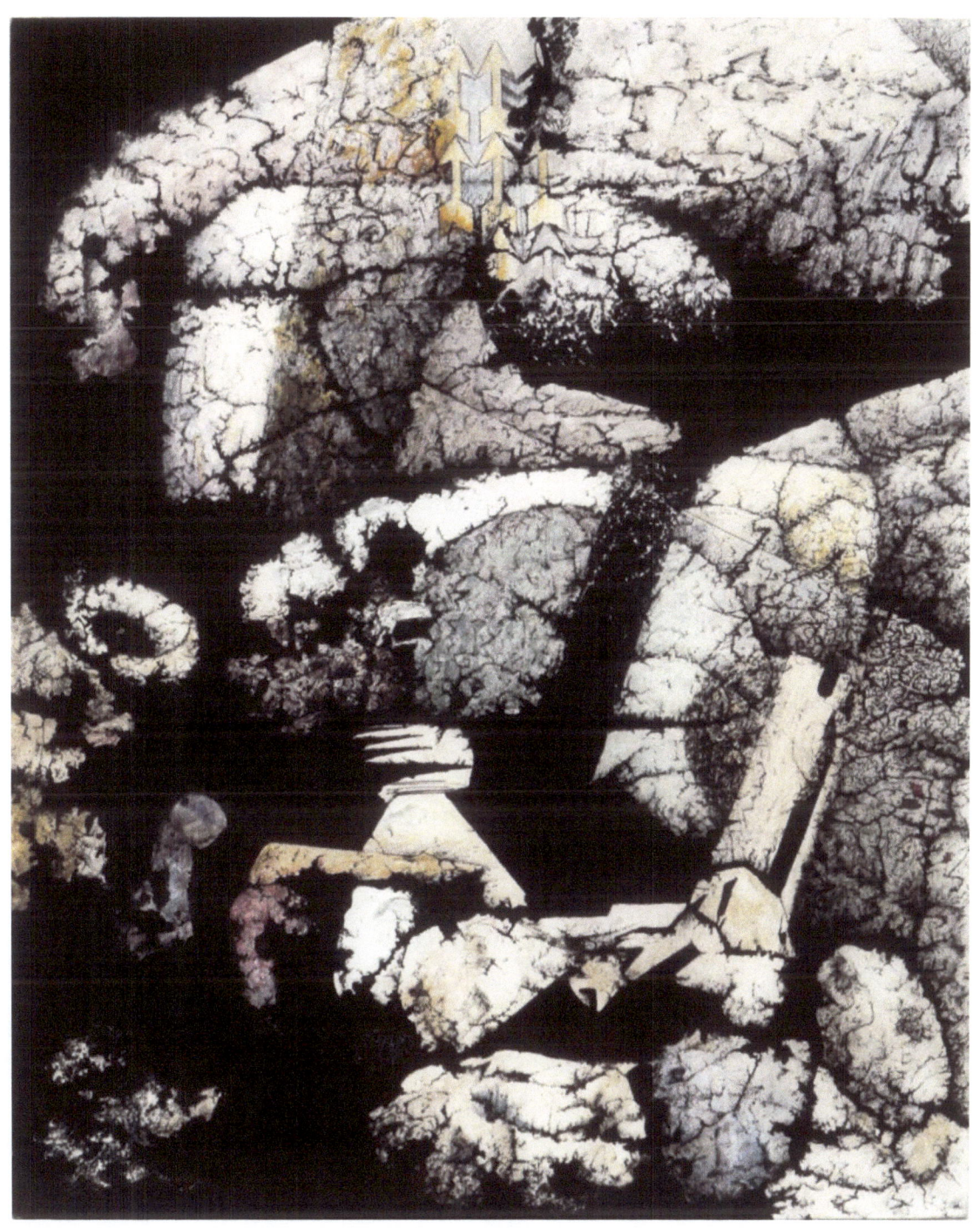

PHENOUMENON TANKA

1977 - 1984
Oil on Canvas
48" x 72"

Vytas may have chosen the word Tanka in the title because of its dual meaning. Not only is it a genre of classical Japanese poetry but is also a Tibetan religious painting or tapestry. A Tanka poem consists of 31 syllables written in 5 lines. The first and third lines have 5 syllables; the others have 7. The word, translated into English means song. Tibetan Tankas are extremely complex, down to attribution of meaning to color. White generally means peace and compassion and a particular shade of green stands for effective activity. Phenoumenon is a word Vytas coined to express the merging of the words phenomenon and noumenon. So, this is a very complex title as befits this complicated composition. No matter which meaning we choose; poem, song, or religious iconography, it is incredibly beautiful.

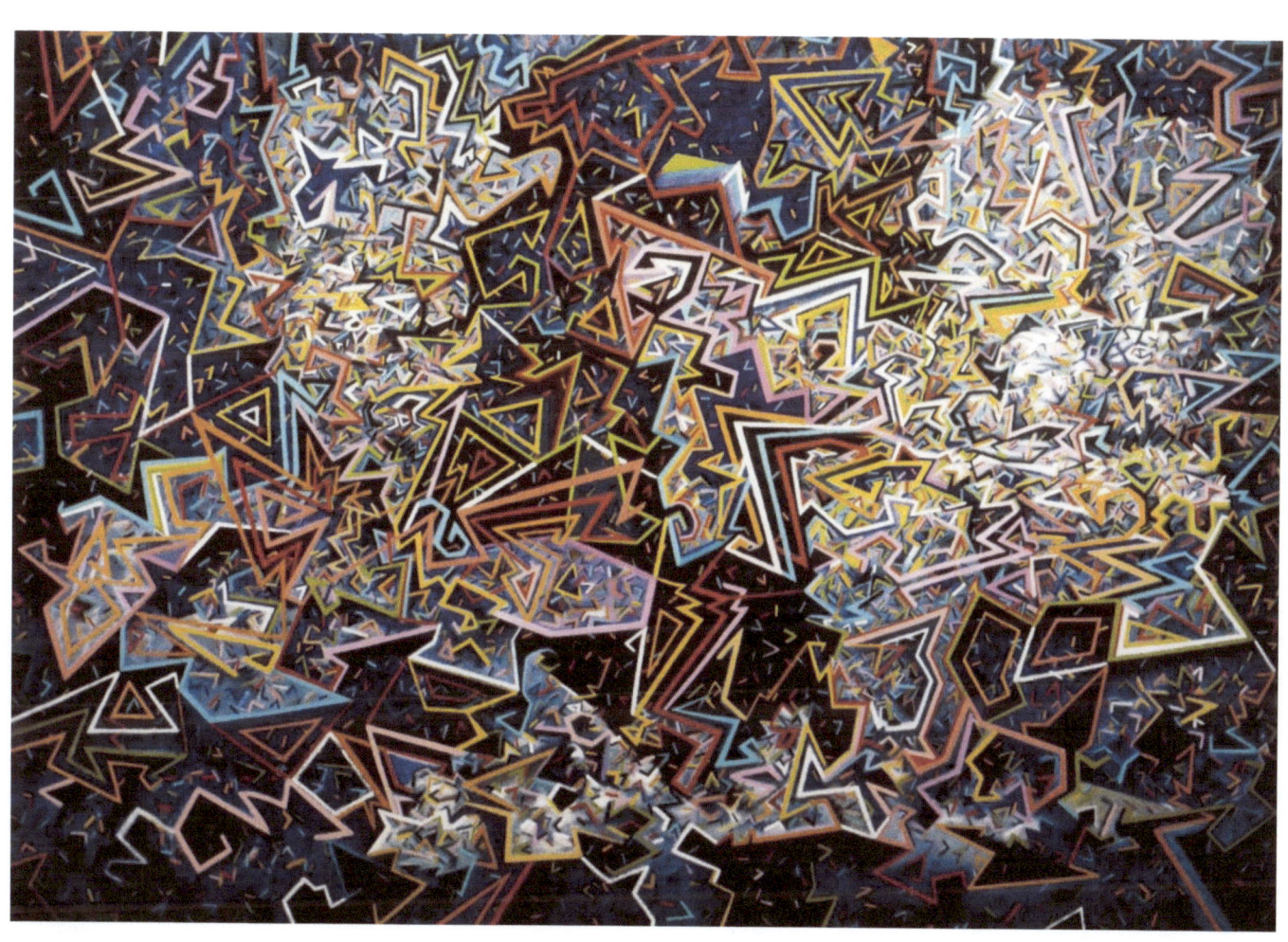

WIND GARDEN

1978 - 1981
Oil on Canvas
48" x 72"
Collection of Lithuanian Museum of Art
Vilnius, Lithuania

Like wind, these shapes flow into and upon each other; triangular breezes move against a darkened sky as though a storm is at hand. Embedded triangles nest inside mother and father forms and beautiful transparencies speak to the invisibility of wind. Wind must be experienced with all the senses. The scent of moving air is like that of rain; unique, delicious beyond reason. We breathe it in deeply, heading west on a fair wind.

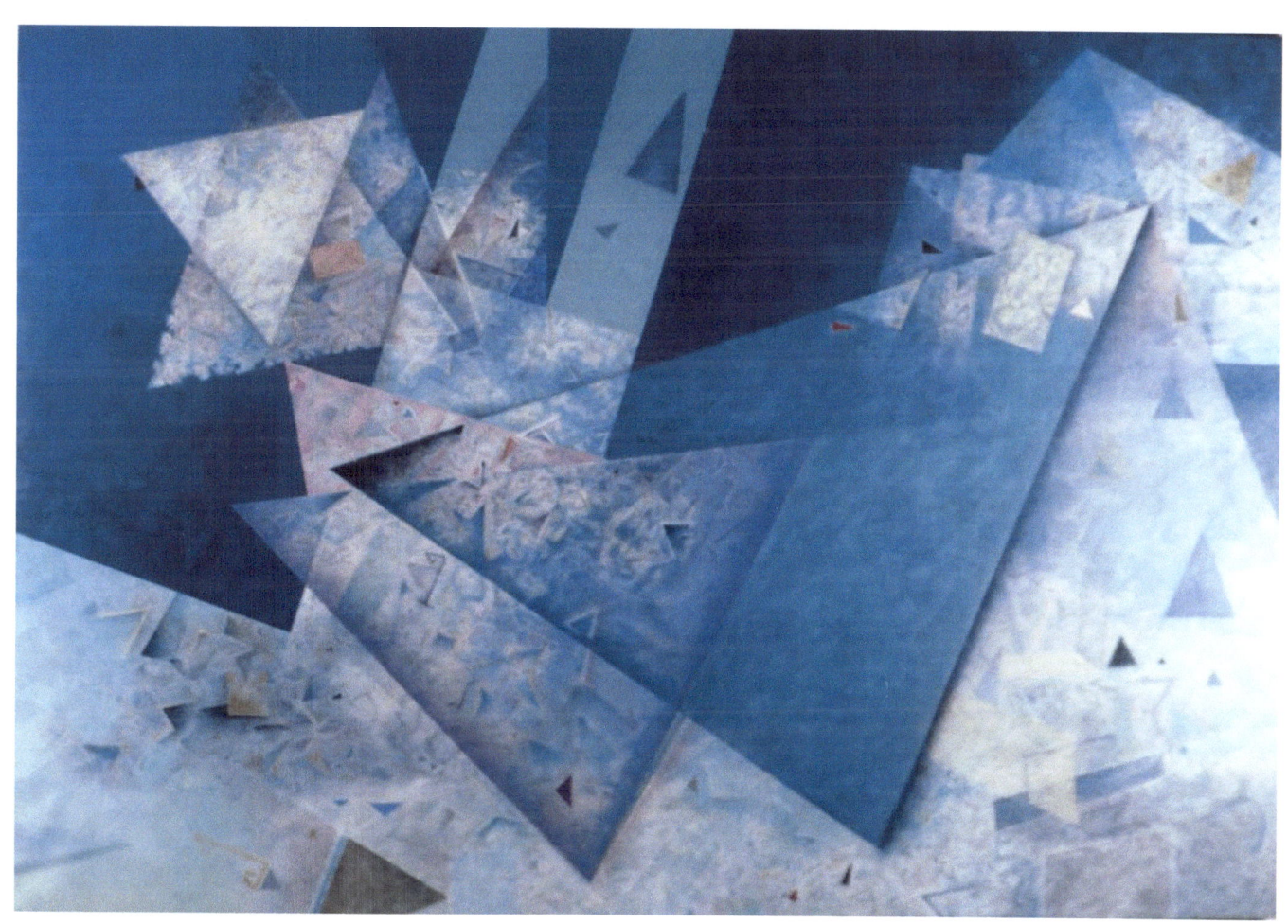

ROMANCE

1983
Oil on Canvas
18" x 14"

The inner movement of dancers has been disclosed. The shapes dance without moving as they define deep spaces within and without. They hold their positions quietly and relate to each other as though they have just met. There is great movement but no change in the shapes. Our eyes provide the movement as we join in this strange *pas de deux*.

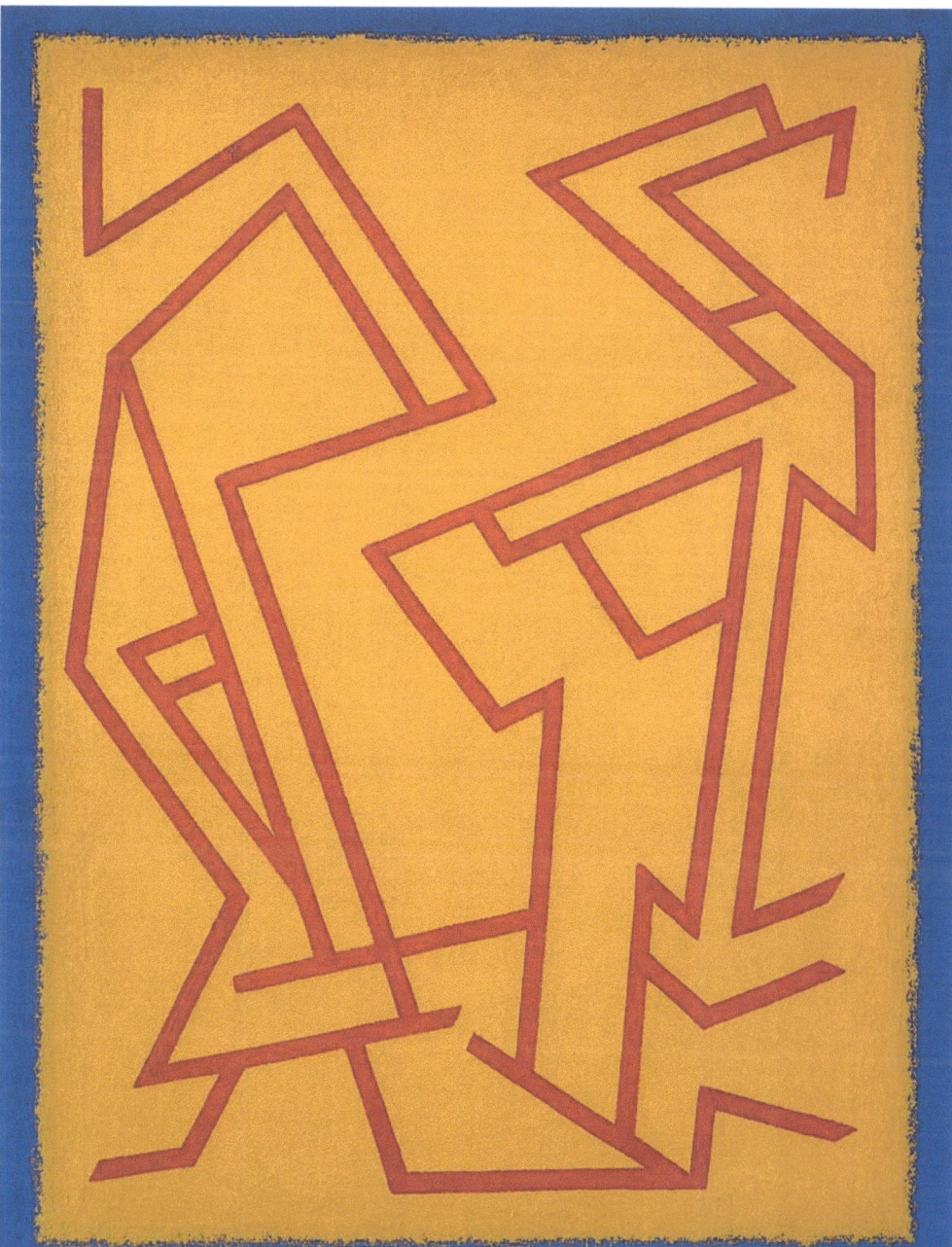

FAMILY

1983
Oil on Canvas
18" x 14"

This painting has been choreographed so that we can see an entire *Corps de Ballet* in action. There is ample interplay between lines and spaces to give the illusion of many separate movements. The totality is one of measured freedom. Music is made inside the parameters of an octave and this blue ballet is confined in a frame measuring 18" x 14".

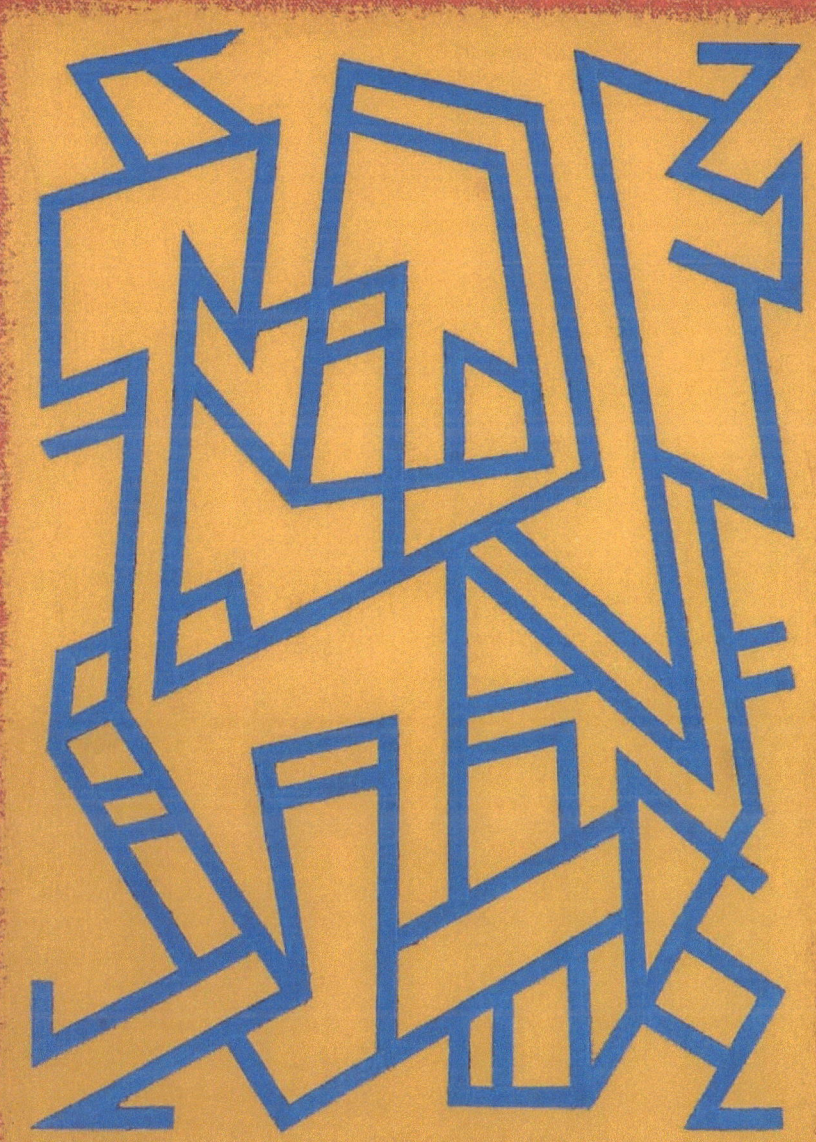

ARRANGEMENT

1983
Oil on Canvas
30" x 24"

The composition, angular and simple in rudimentary parts, is made complex by the way Vytas has placed the disparate elements. This causes it to move internally as if wound tight like a clock or music box. The color slaps us, sweeping from every direction at once and like time ticking forward, or a movement of forgotten music, we are transported into the arrangement.

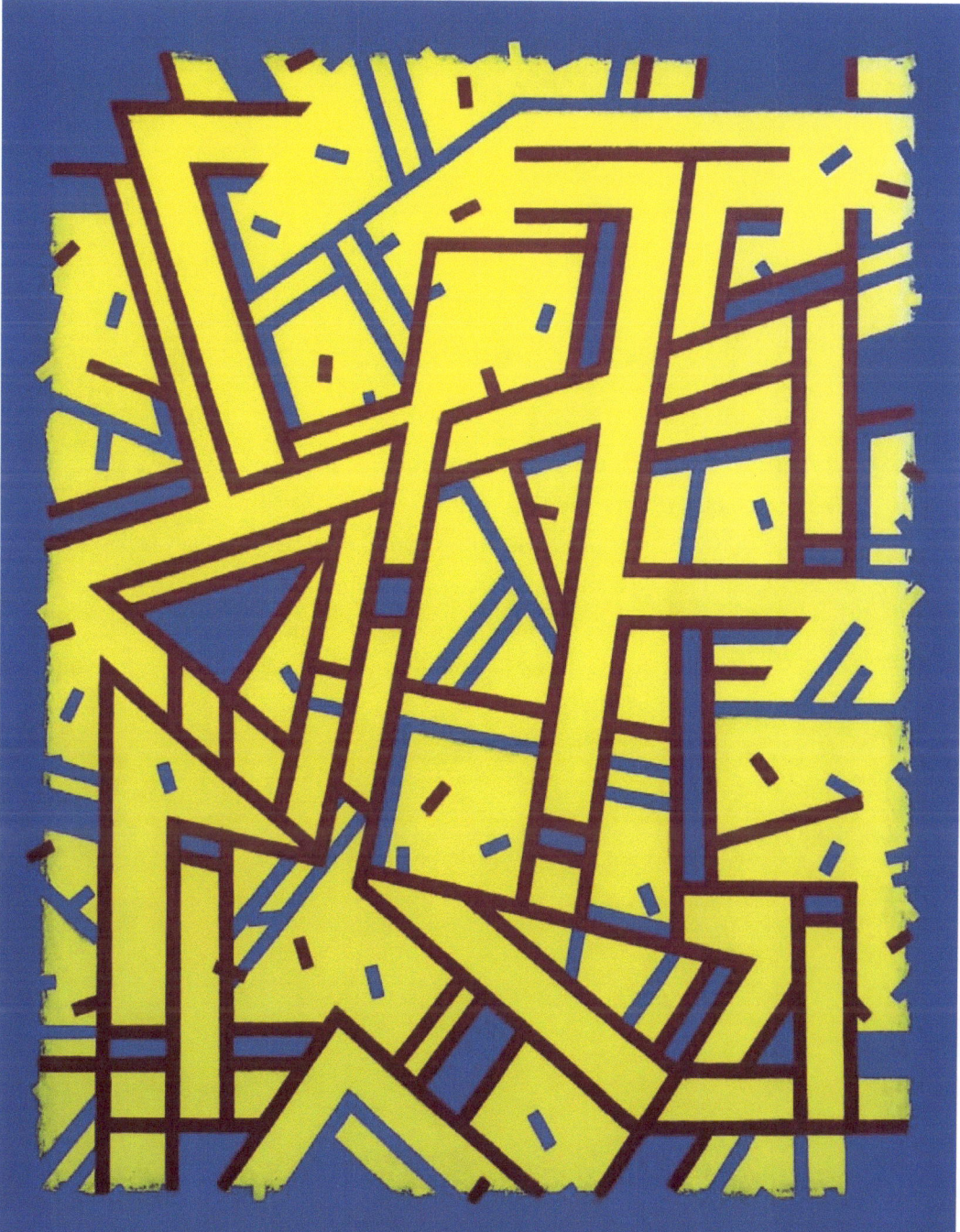

KINT

2000 - 2001
Oil on Canvas
18" x 14"

In contrast to many of his other geometrics, Vytas has added more color to this painting. It looks like he has painted in code and my eyes are trying to unlock the secret. This may speak to abstract dreams of basket weavers or women who create designs in rugs. It could be a modern hieroglyph to leave for a far future when people will discover this piece and get lost in its mystery.

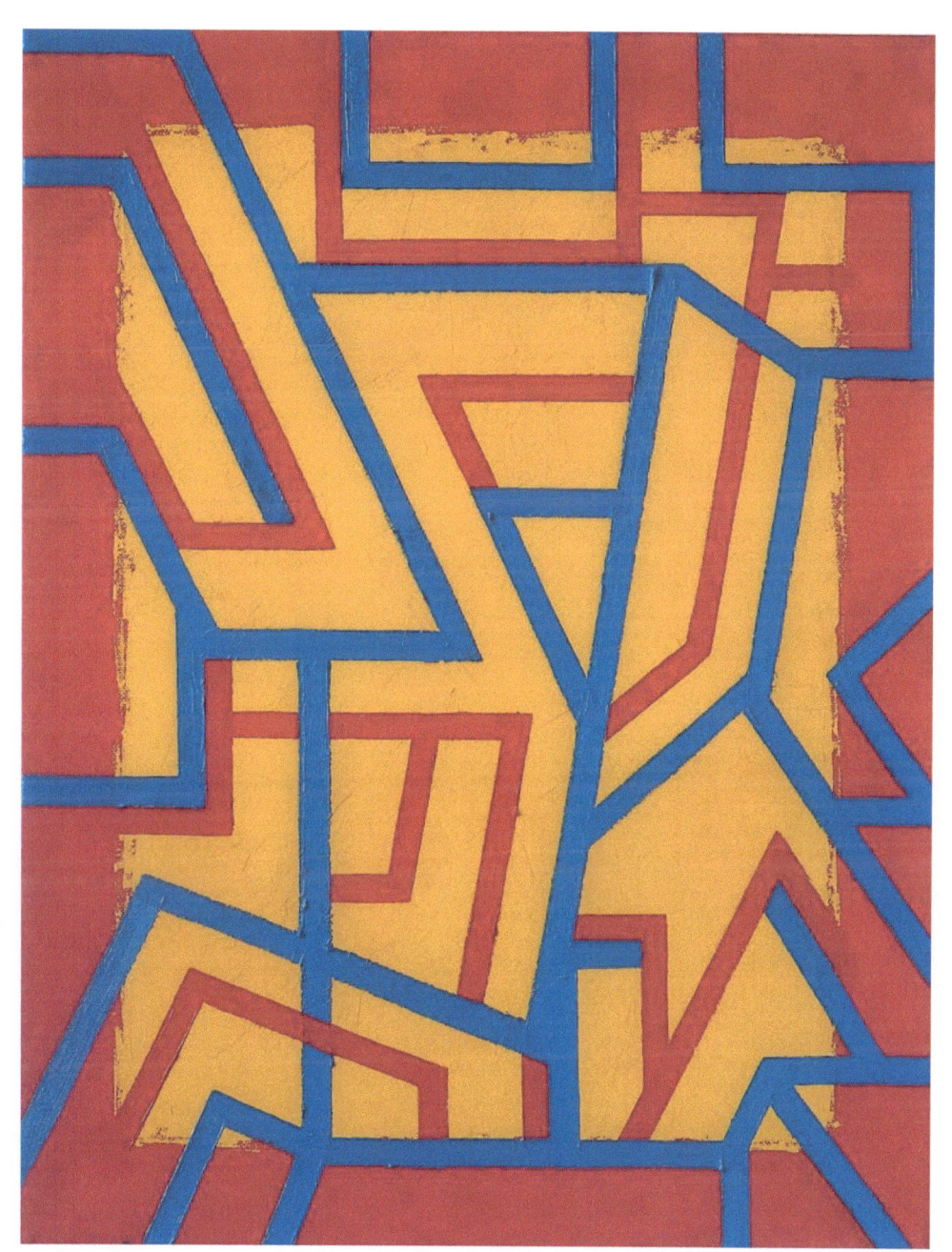

MUDU ABUDU

1983 - 1984
Oil on Aluminum Cutout
96" x 104"

Vytas considers this the masterpiece of his cutout works. They differ from other wall art in that he uses the wall itself as part of the piece. Unlike *bas relief* which extends out into space, his work creates a dimensional effect by using geometrics and meaningful juxtapositions of the disparate pieces of the whole artwork. He manages a third dimension upon a flat surface. This technique, which he invented, maximizes relationships of negative and positive space.

This particular piece is grand in scale, measuring 96" x 104" and is replete with hundreds of tiny designs and figures. He cut the design by hand into aluminum with a jigsaw then added the embellishments with paint. The detail and beautiful colors should be seen in real life to fully appreciate the workmanship. Several examples follow so you will have a sense of these enchanting works.

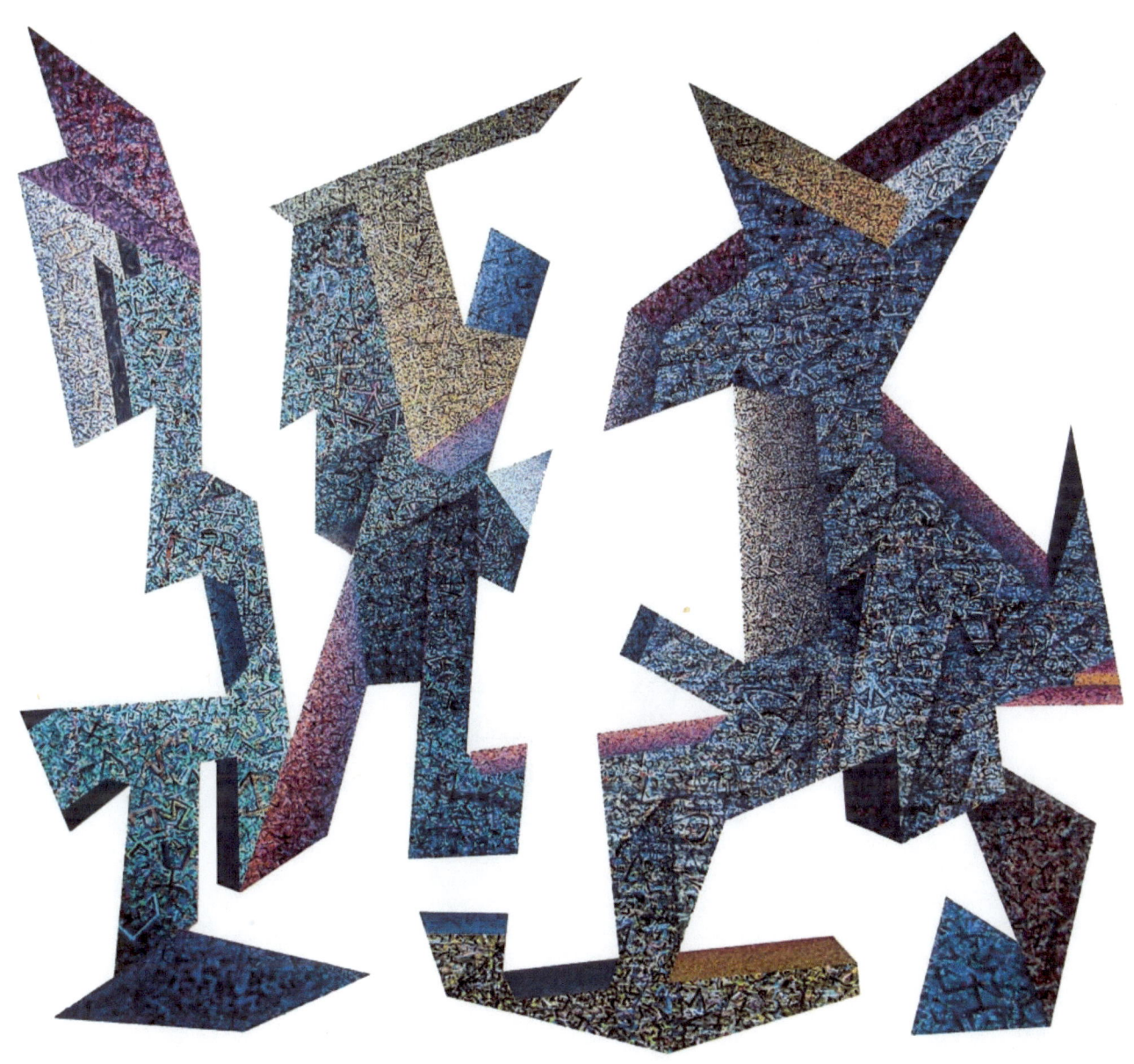

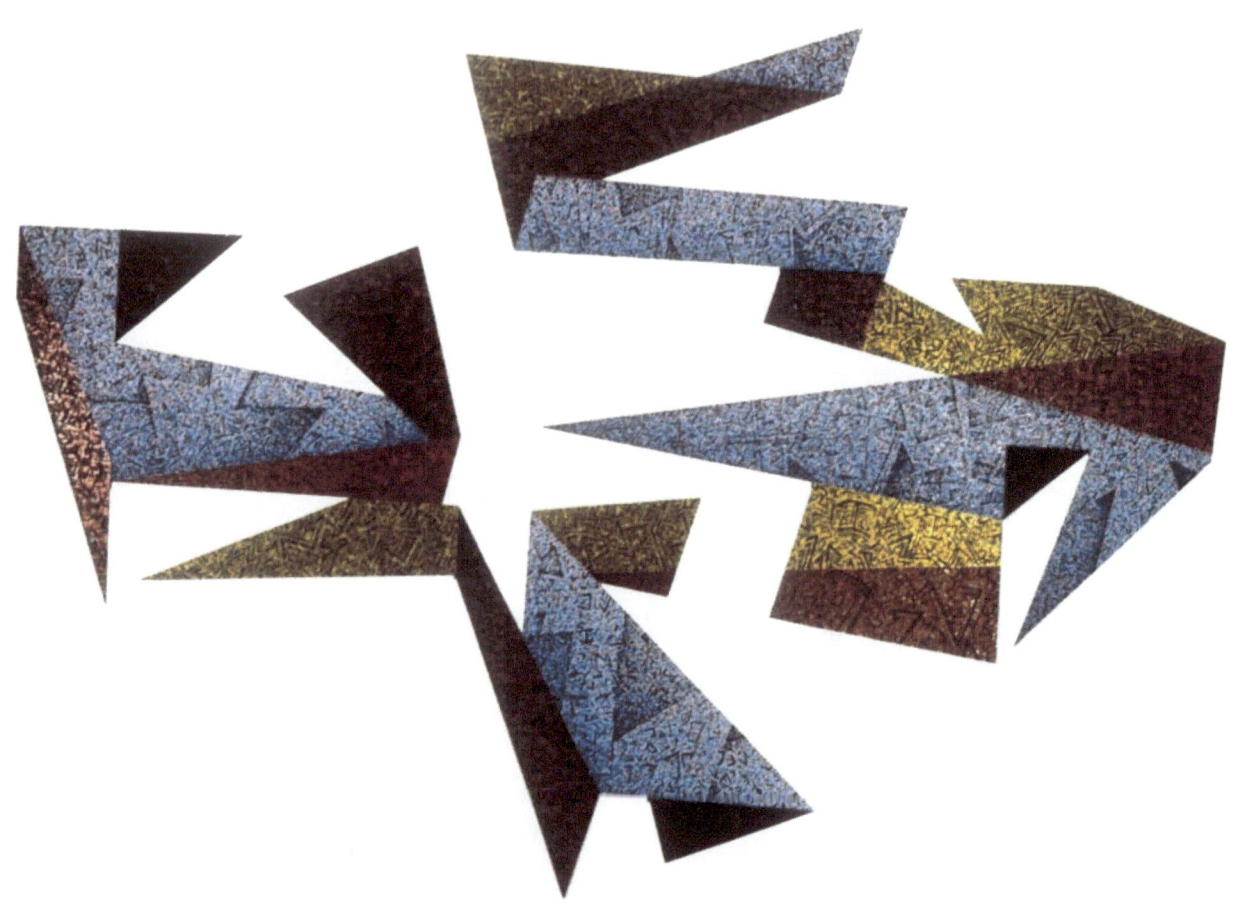

PURUSHKA

1983 - 1984
Oil on Aluminum Cutout
48″ x 72″

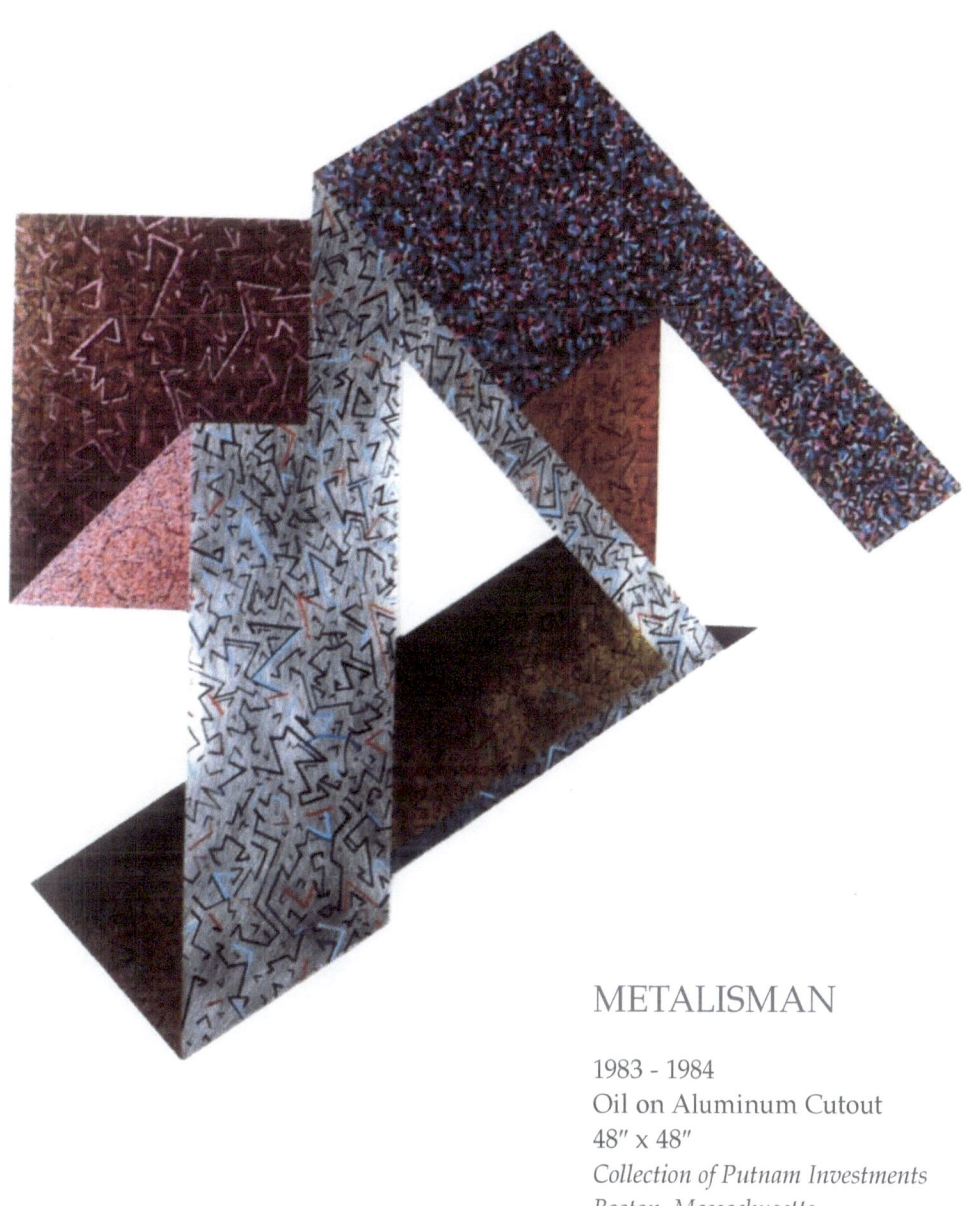

METALISMAN

1983 - 1984
Oil on Aluminum Cutout
48" x 48"
Collection of Putnam Investments
Boston, Massachusetts

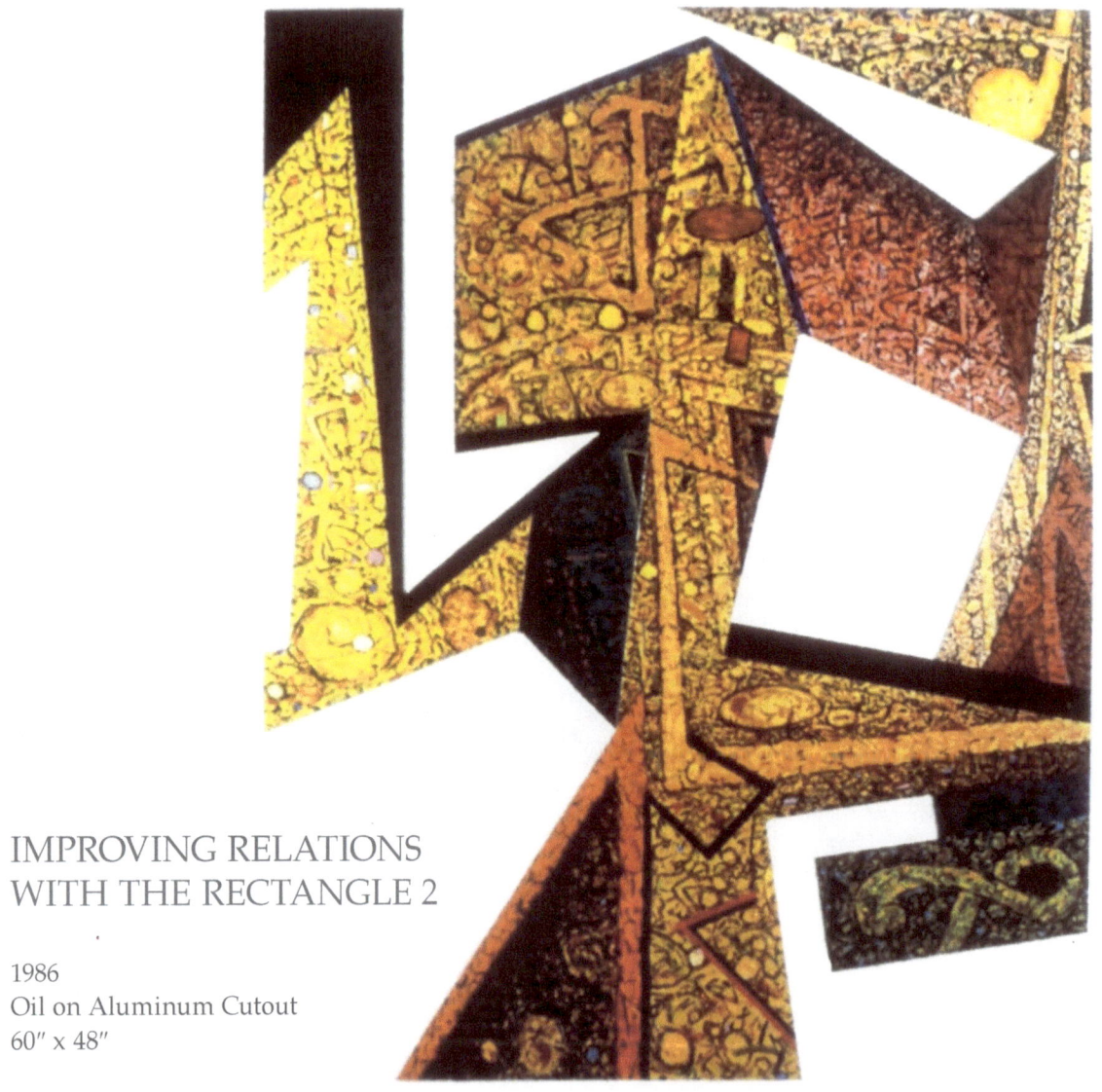

IMPROVING RELATIONS
WITH THE RECTANGLE 2

1986
Oil on Aluminum Cutout
60" x 48"

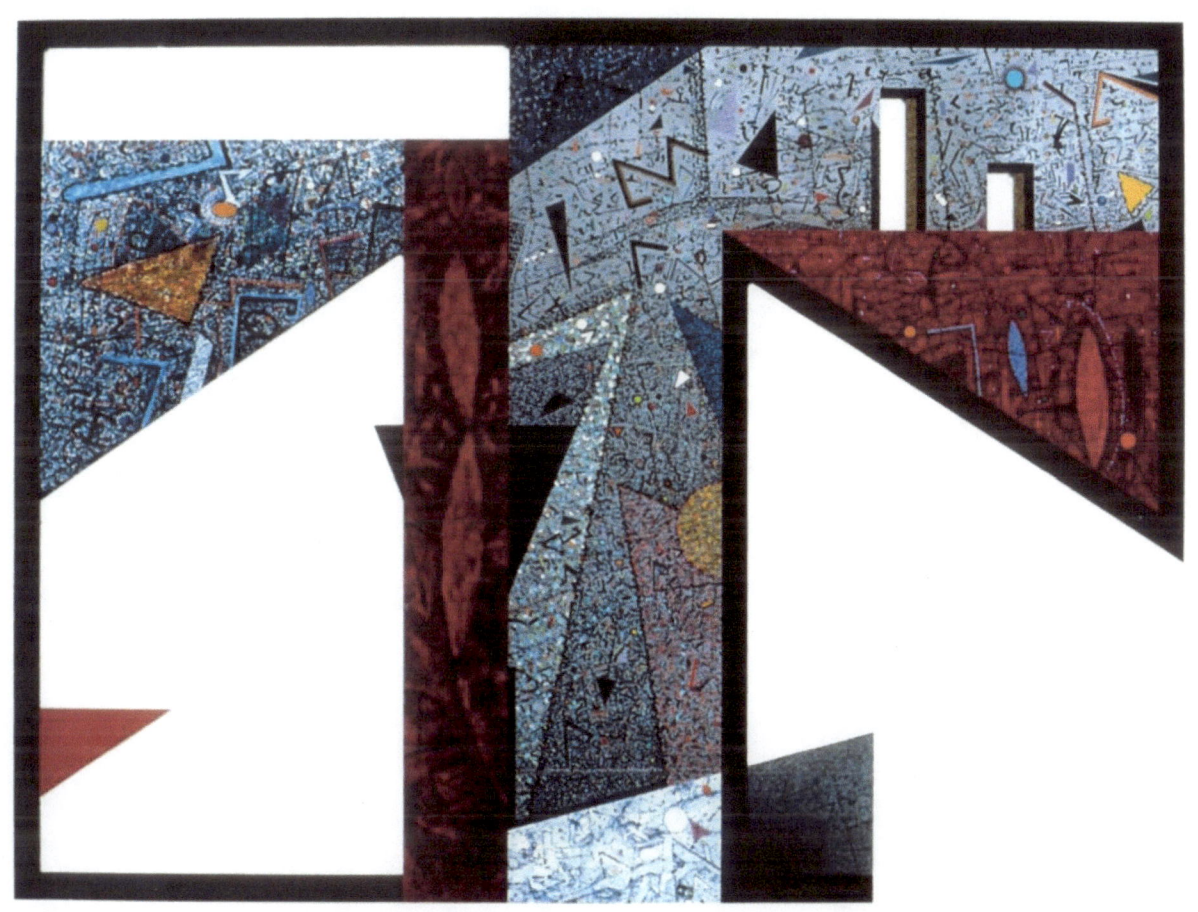

IMPROVING RELATIONS
WITH THE RECTANGLE 7

1987
Oil on Aluminum Cutout
60" x 84"
Collection of Boston Globe Newspaper Company
Boston, Massachusetts

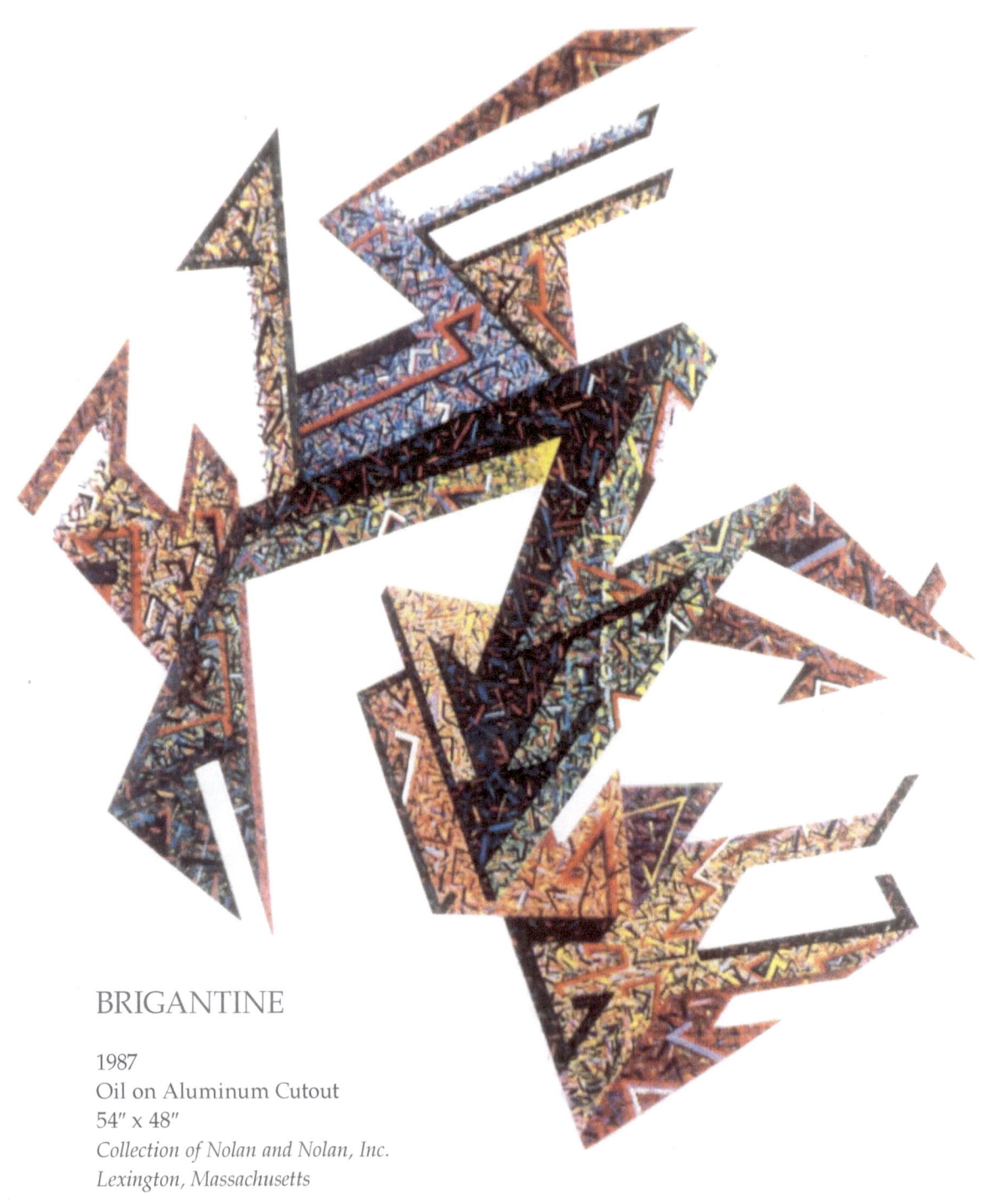

BRIGANTINE

1987
Oil on Aluminum Cutout
54" x 48"
Collection of Nolan and Nolan, Inc.
Lexington, Massachusetts

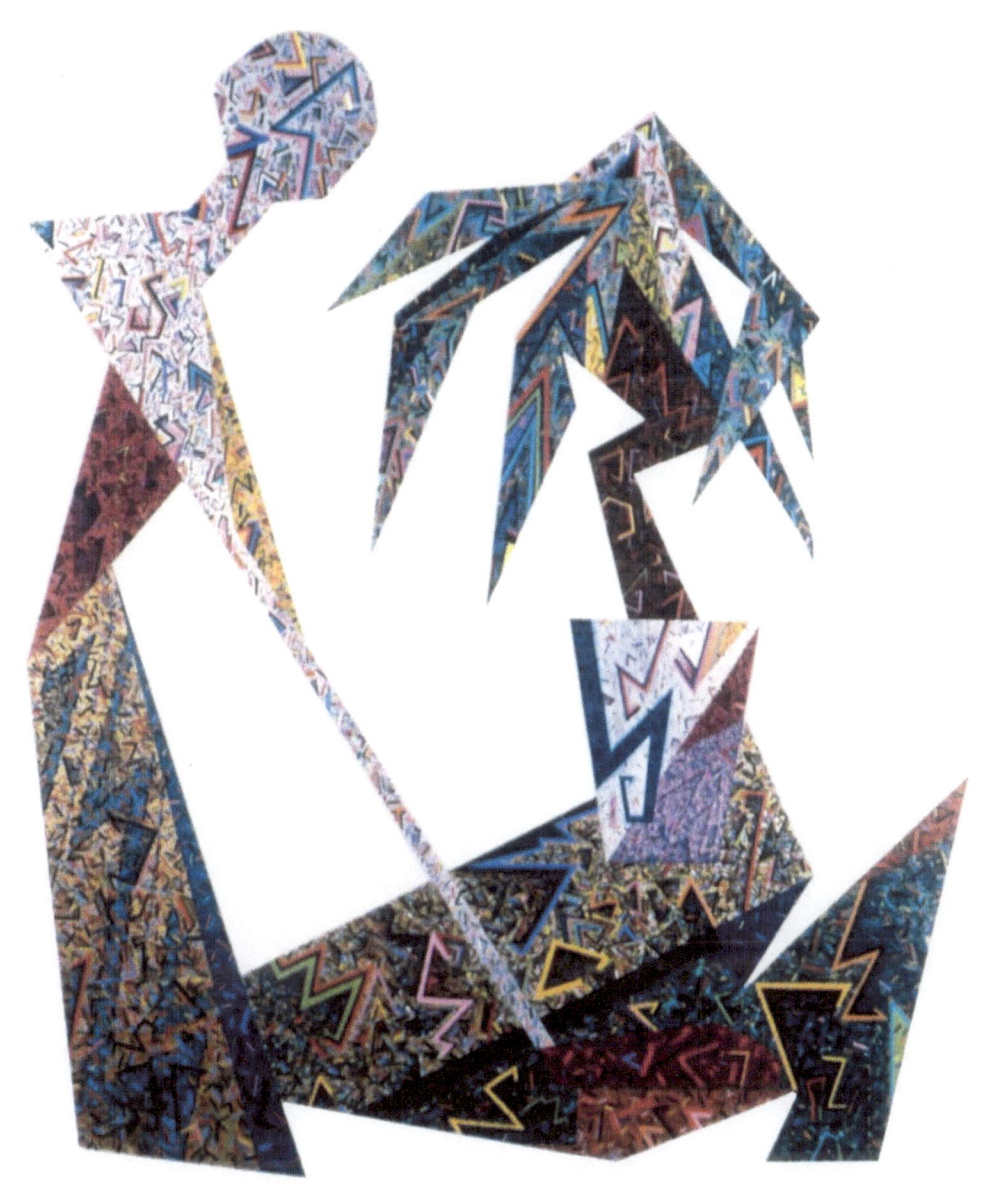

DOMICILE

1988
Oil on Aluminum Cutout
70" x 60"

BURNING KARMA

1979 - 1983
Oil on Canvas
48" x 64"

Although this is one of his earlier works, it could well be put alongside his recent work with little evidence of a great time interval. It attests to the notion that Vytas' particular vision was intact from the beginning and he has been allowing that vision to unfold over time. Each piece he does is singular, complete and unique but the undergirding essence is always the same: brilliance.

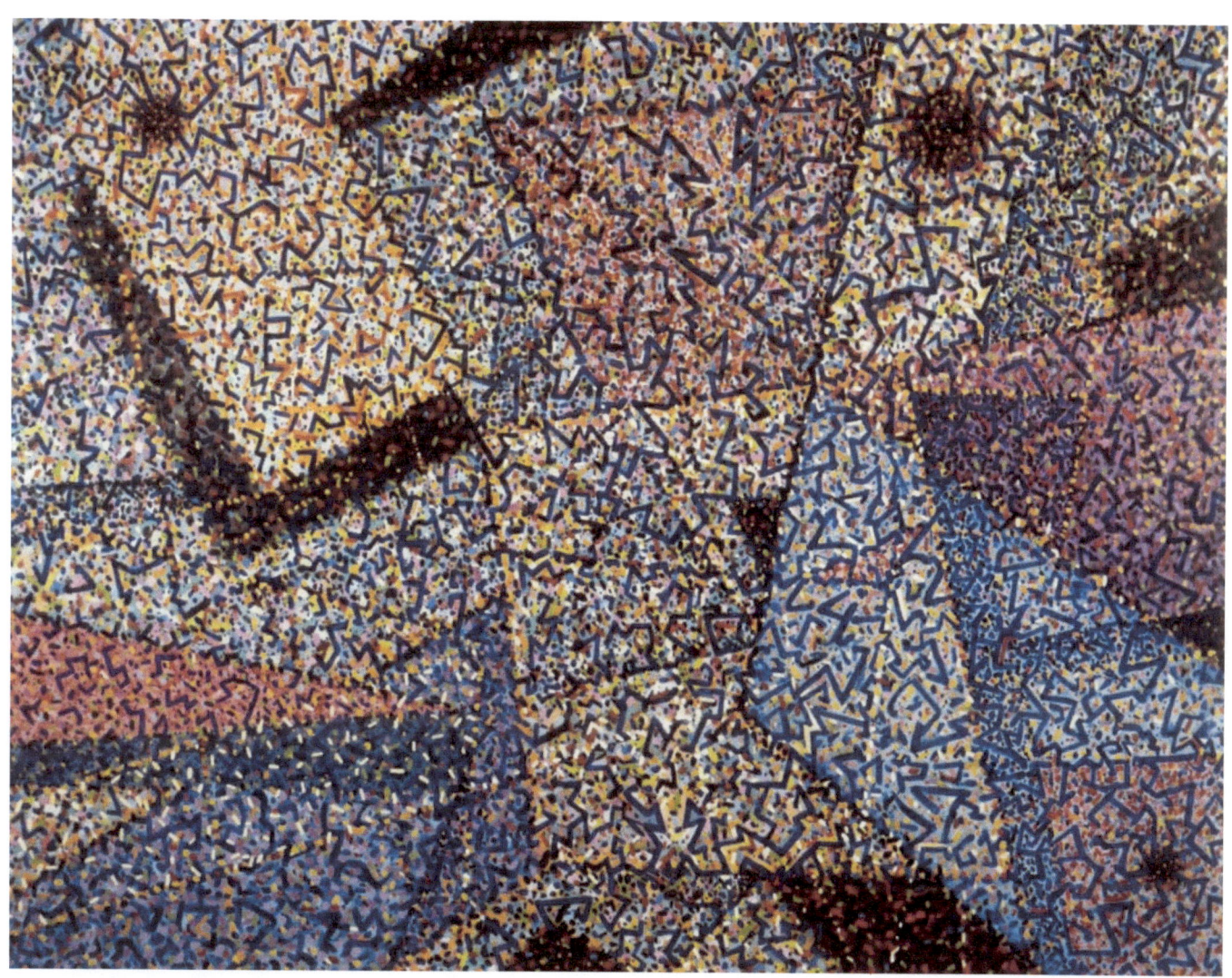

TOURENDOT

1991 - 1995
Acrylic on Paper
30" x 22"

The title Tourendot is a play on Puccini's opera Turandot, wherein hapless suitors have to solve three riddles in order to win the Princess Turandot. Vytas has created a massive riddle for us here. What are we seeing beyond the face value of colored dots meticulously rendered? Is it a depiction of the great question, "What is the purpose of life?" If so, then it is up to us to look at this beauty head on and decide if there is any need to attach meaning to it.

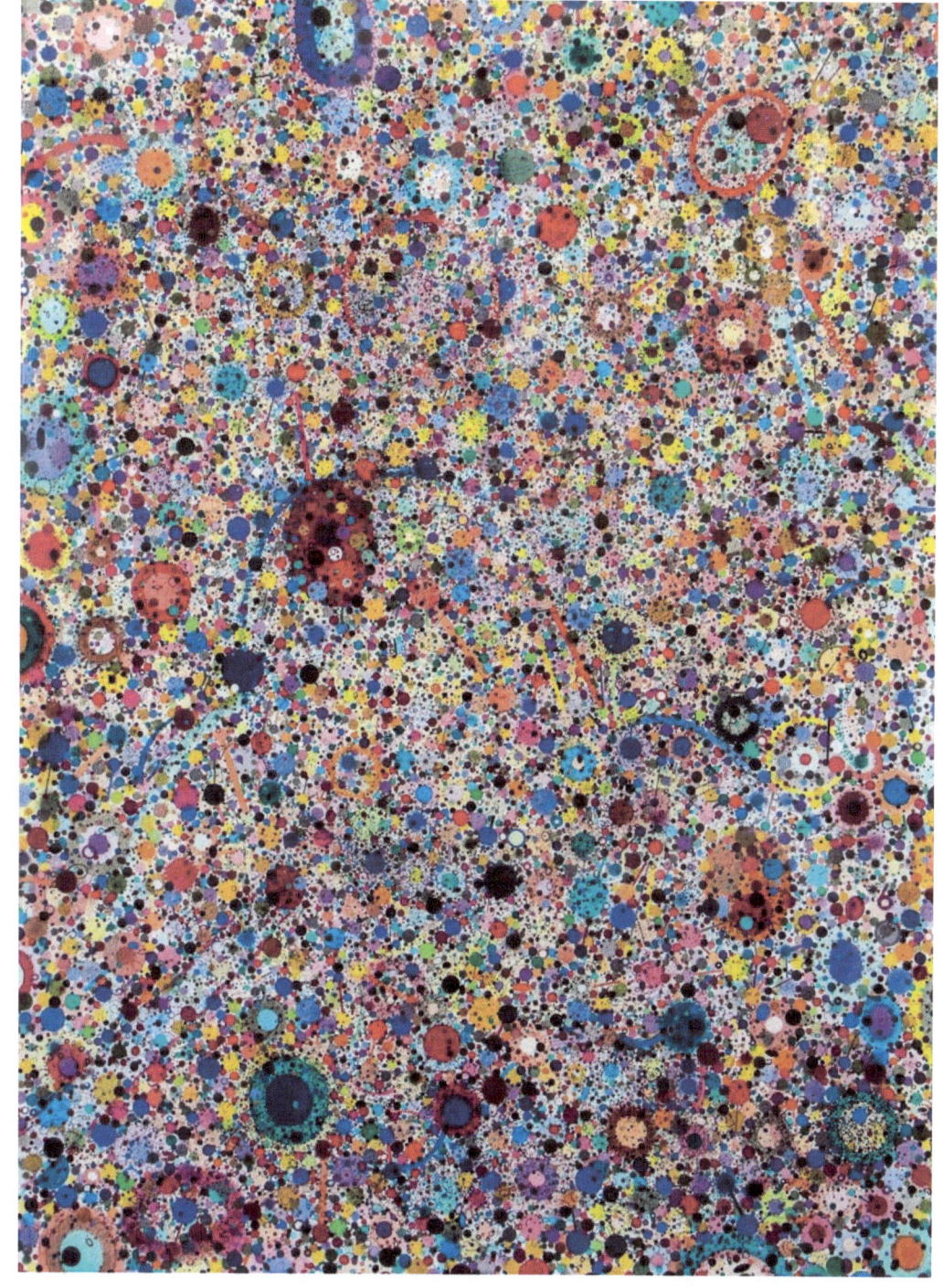

COW SKULL WITH CACTI

1993 - 1994
Oil on Canvas
24" x 20"

Vytas has brought Cubism to a new frontier, the Southwest. We easily identify the flat leaves of prickly pear, the smooth tall green of saguaro and the dried, whitened skull of a cow. These are all too common subjects in art of the Southwest but Vytas has given them uncommon treatment. There is a freshness imbued within all the jagged cubistic lines and solid forms. We witness, in a novel way, the juxtaposition of life and death in the desert and see deep beauty in the natural cycle.

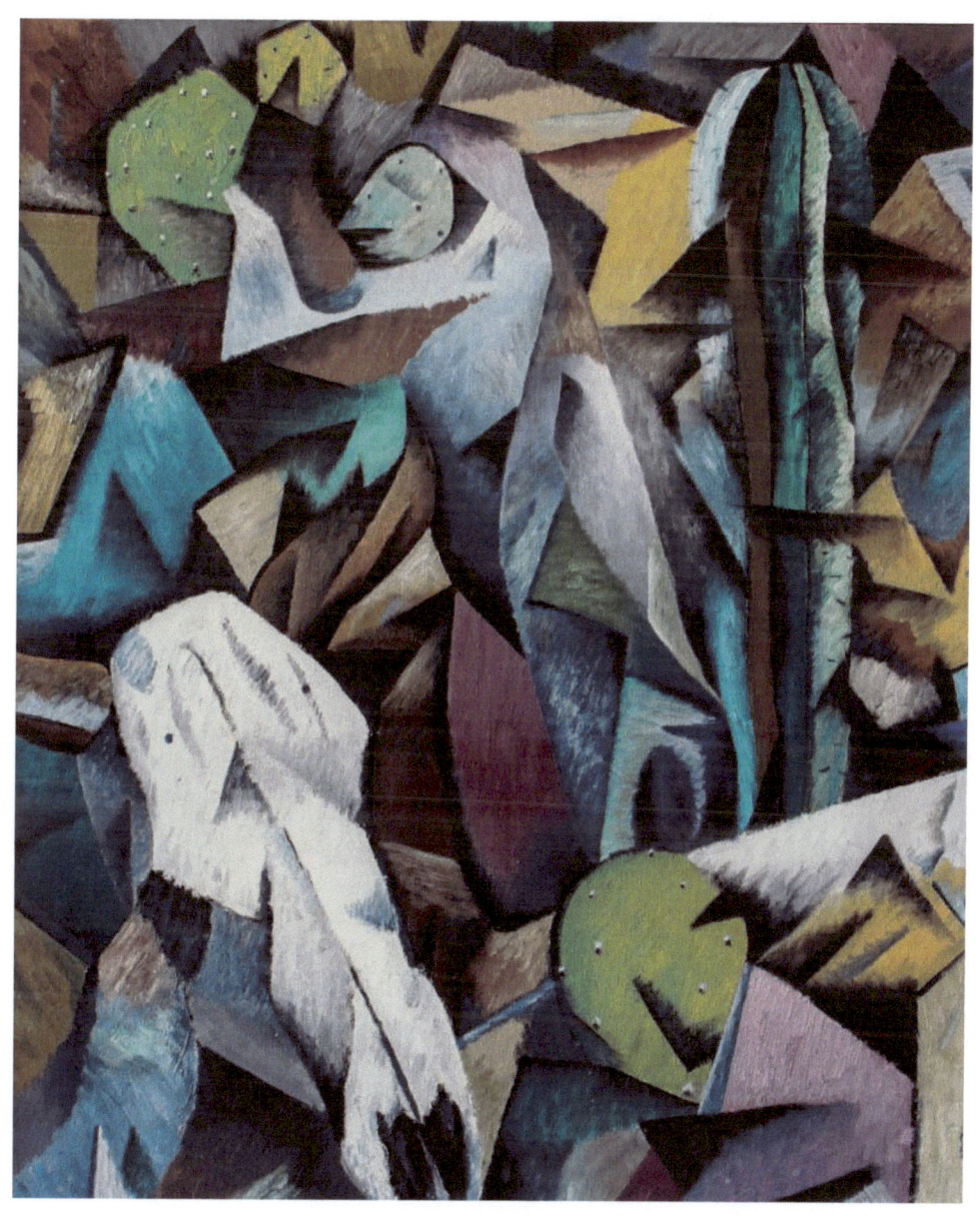

BOOTS AND HAT BY WINDOW

1995
Oil on Canvas
36" x 24"

The color choices are definitely Southwestern. These colors could be made from the dirt, cacti, sage and rock that define the desert. As our eyes scan across the canvas we perceive the boots and hat, as they become forms we recognize. They create a composition of familiar items but are presented in an unfamiliar way. Vytas has taken the ordinary and depicted it in such a way that it seems we are looking through a magic kaleidoscope.

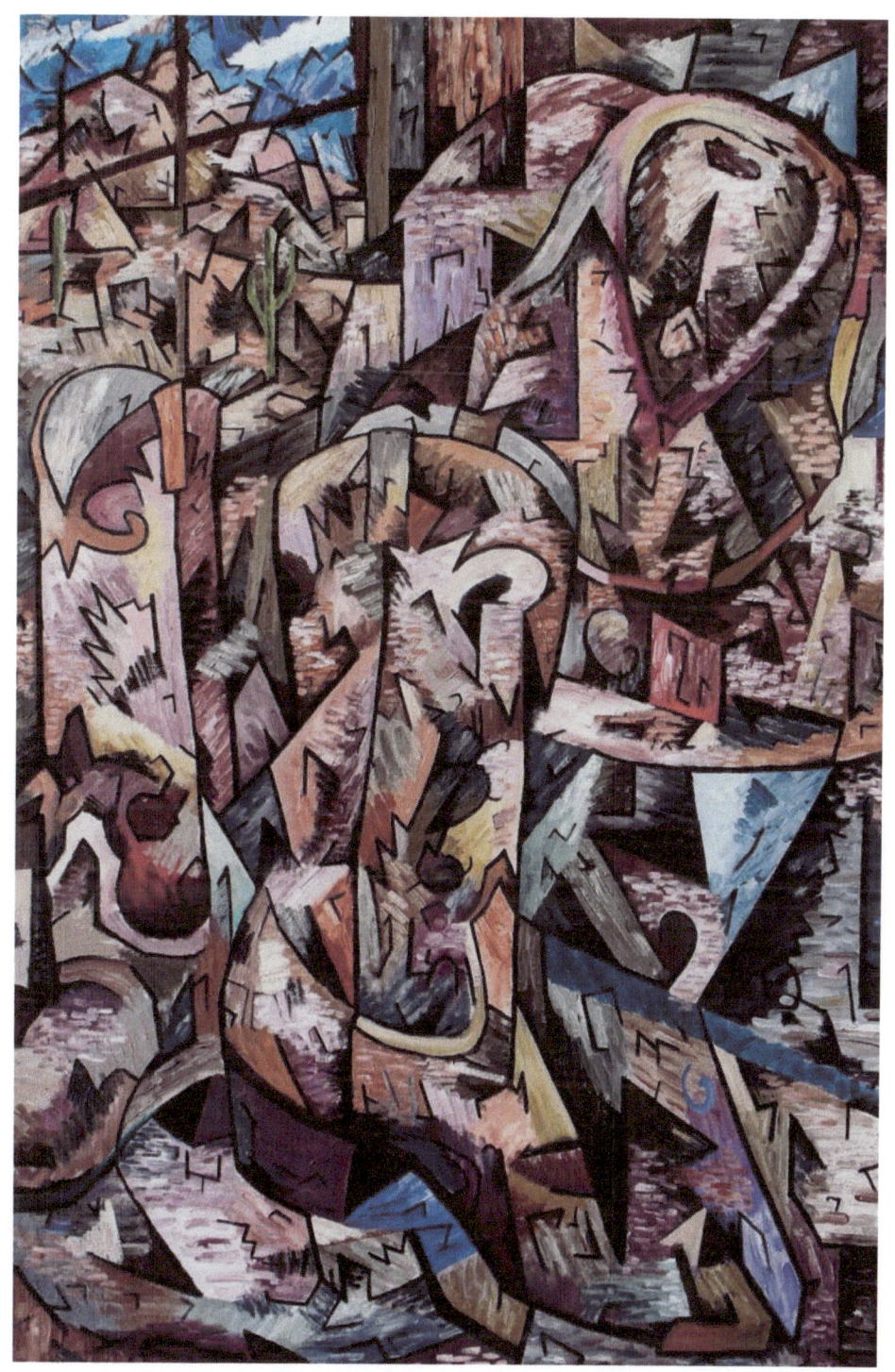

JACKRABBIT BY SAGUARO

1995
Oil on Canvas
40" x 30"

The jackrabbit and saguaro are familiar life in the desert. The cubist style of this work moves them just slightly into unfamiliar territory. Survival is difficult where little grows and rain is rare yet this creature is standing firmly rooted in a stance of strength. This is not what generally comes to mind when we think of rabbits. Instead of soft and cute he looks heroic, even a bit menacing. He owns this territory and will not be moved from it. We are resigned to viewing him from outside his country.

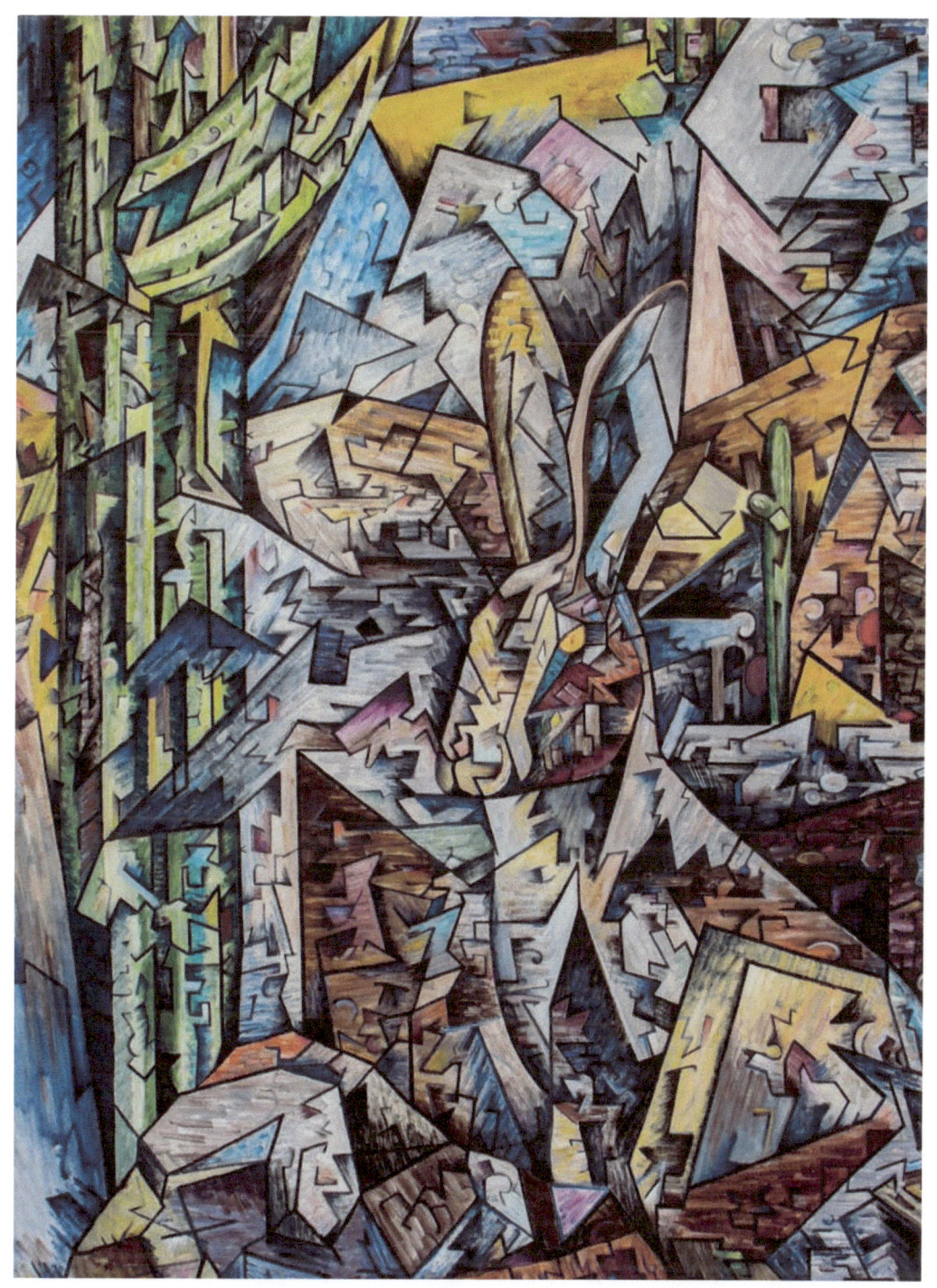

MARE AND FOAL

1995 - 1999
Oil on Canvas
24" x 24"

There is, in this painting, a universal element of the tender love mothers have for their young. The mare's nostril is slightly flared as though she is taking in the scent of her newborn, ensuring she will always recognize her own. Vytas depicts her as she nuzzles the baby with such tenderness that it continues sleeping. It is surprising how much softness is conveyed despite all the very strong straight and angled lines in the painting. It is brilliant work.

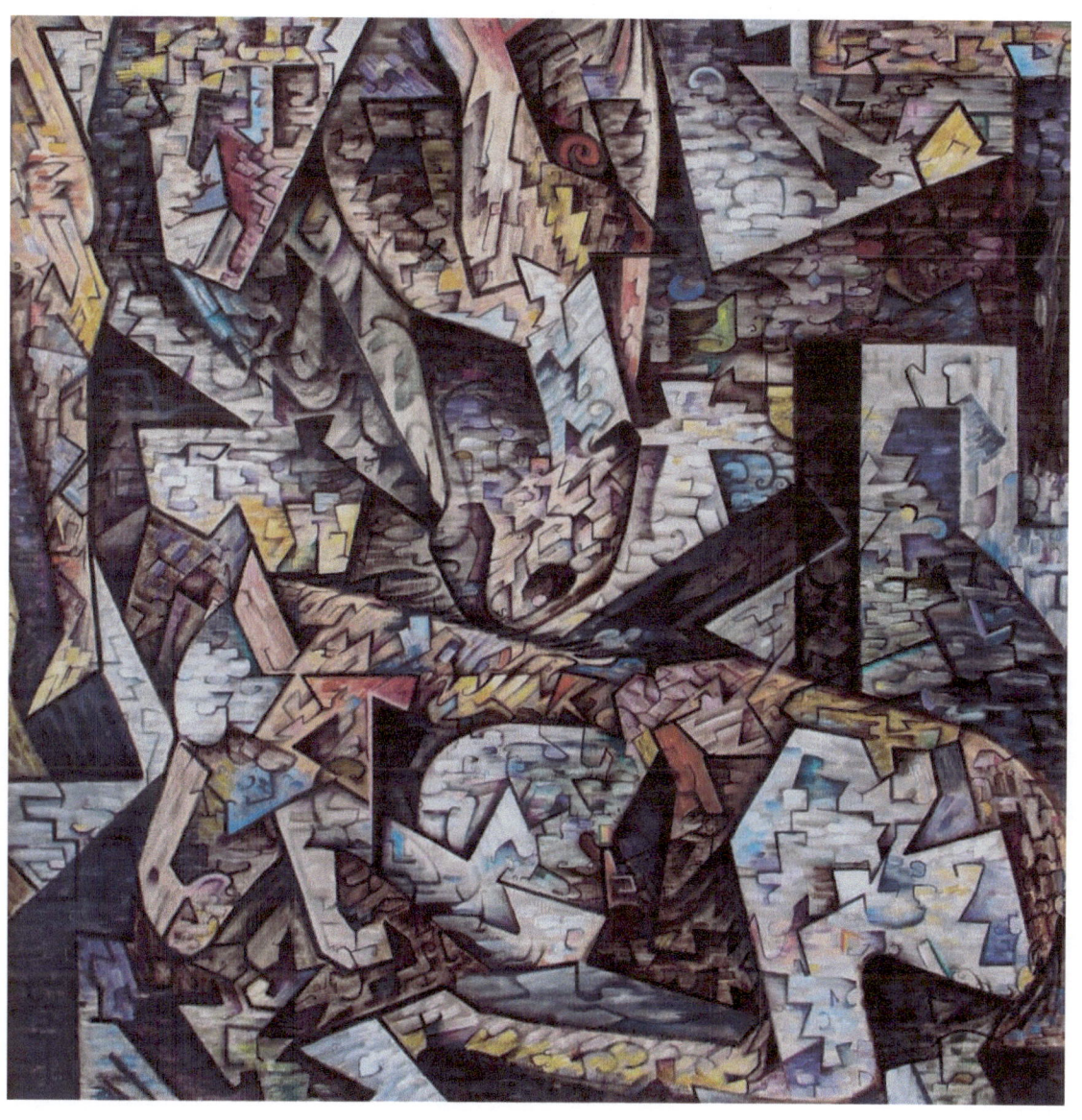

PORTRAIT OF ALLAN HART
AS "CLEM HARPER"

1998 - 2001
Oil on Canvas
30" x 24"

Hidden but not concealed, the artist is viewing the outside world trying to put it into a new order. Piece by piece the aura surrounding him almost fits into place and yet there is tremendous space available around each separate part. Even the gaze of the subject looks into a far future, where everything dreamed of will fall into a perfect pattern. His eyes pull us into that quest.

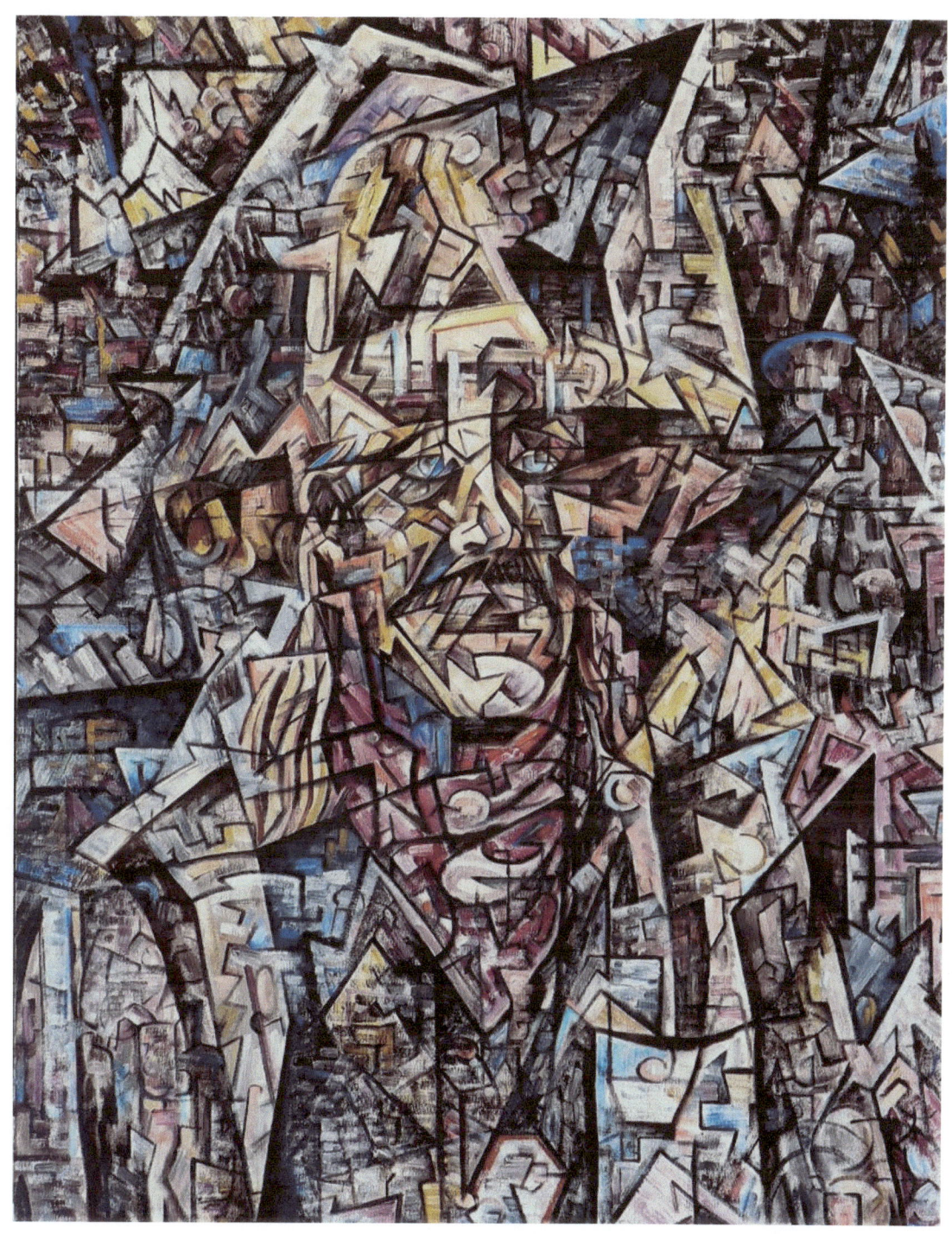

KING'S THRONE
IN MONUMENT VALLEY

1997 - 2007
Oil over Acrylic on Canvas
60" x 48"
Collection of the Lewben Art Foundation
Vilnius, Lithuania

Vytas is practicing architecture and masonry here. The natural formation of rock is transformed in such a way that it looks fabricated, as though the landscape was created by layering rock on rock. Vytas has built the throne and chiseled paint to make a portrait of the king who rules the valley. Ozymandias yet lives in this antique land of bare bones rock and glistening sand.

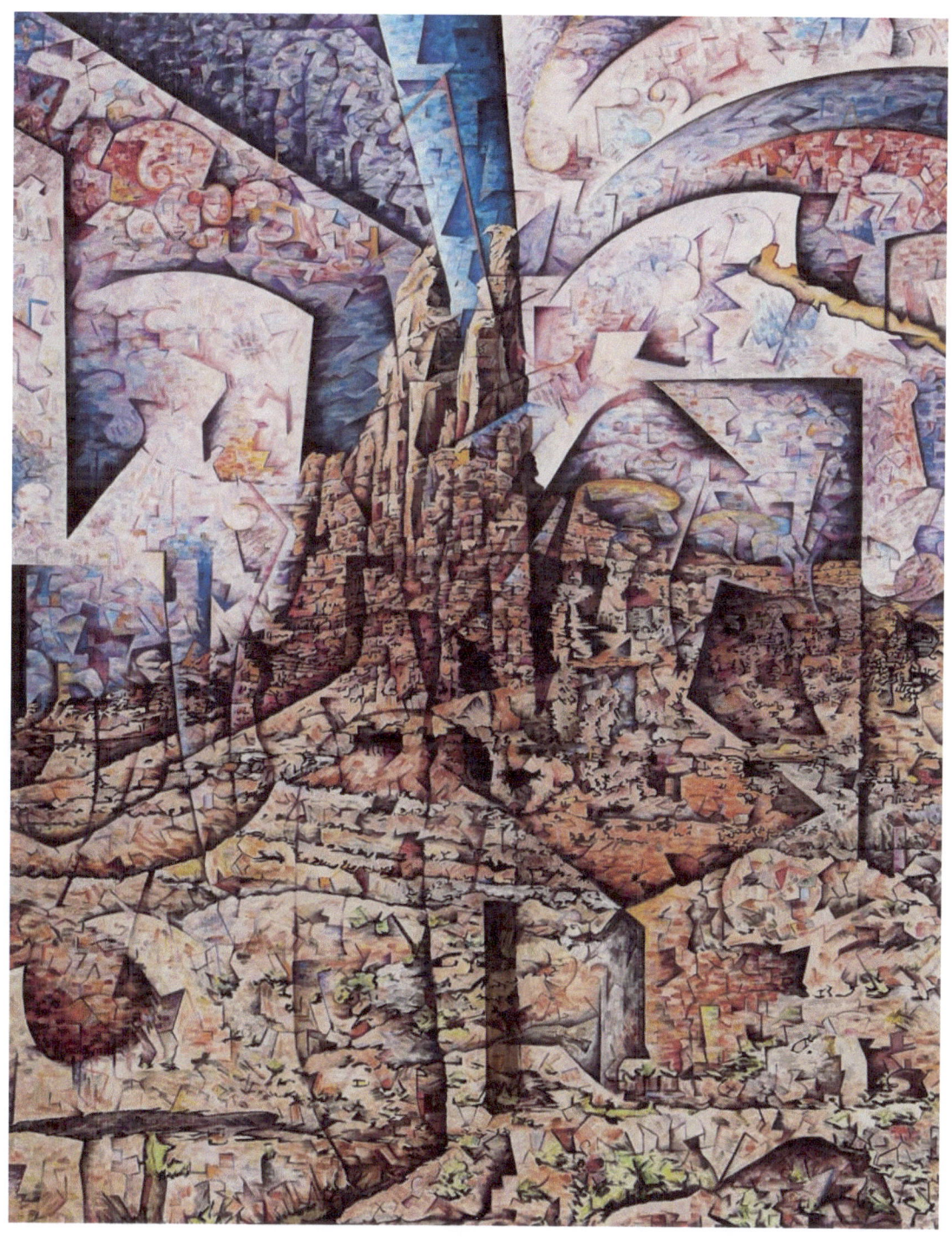

CHIRICAHUA FORMATION

1997 - 2000
Oil on Canvas
48" x 60"

Deep within these shapes reside hints of Native dreams.
Patterns appear and morph into larger patterns creating
beautiful designs such as one might find on ancient
artifacts. It is as if Vytas is recalling hieroglyphs of old
and rendering them here as an homage to holy places.
The stones sing the songs of the ancient ones and they
come close to whisper their secrets in color and form.

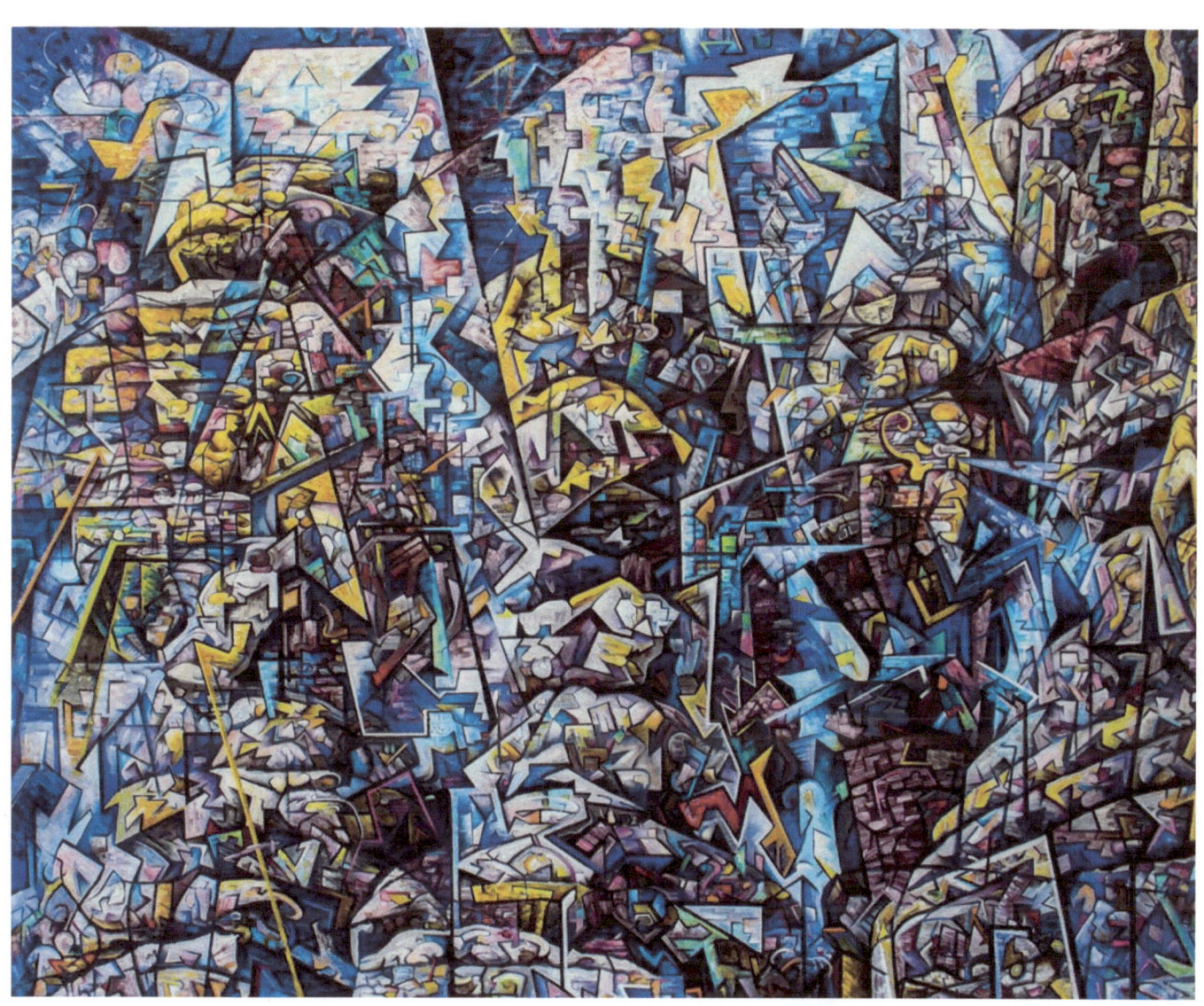

BELL ROCK, SEDONA

1998 - 2008
Oil on Canvas
60" x 60"

Vytas has captured the feel and fabric of an aboriginal reality. The color and relationship of intricate forms could be ancient places revisited as we travel through his painting. It feels like we belong here in a hard rock country. We enter this radiant world sensing the distance separating us from those people who lived before us. This, like all journeys in consciousness, is sacred.

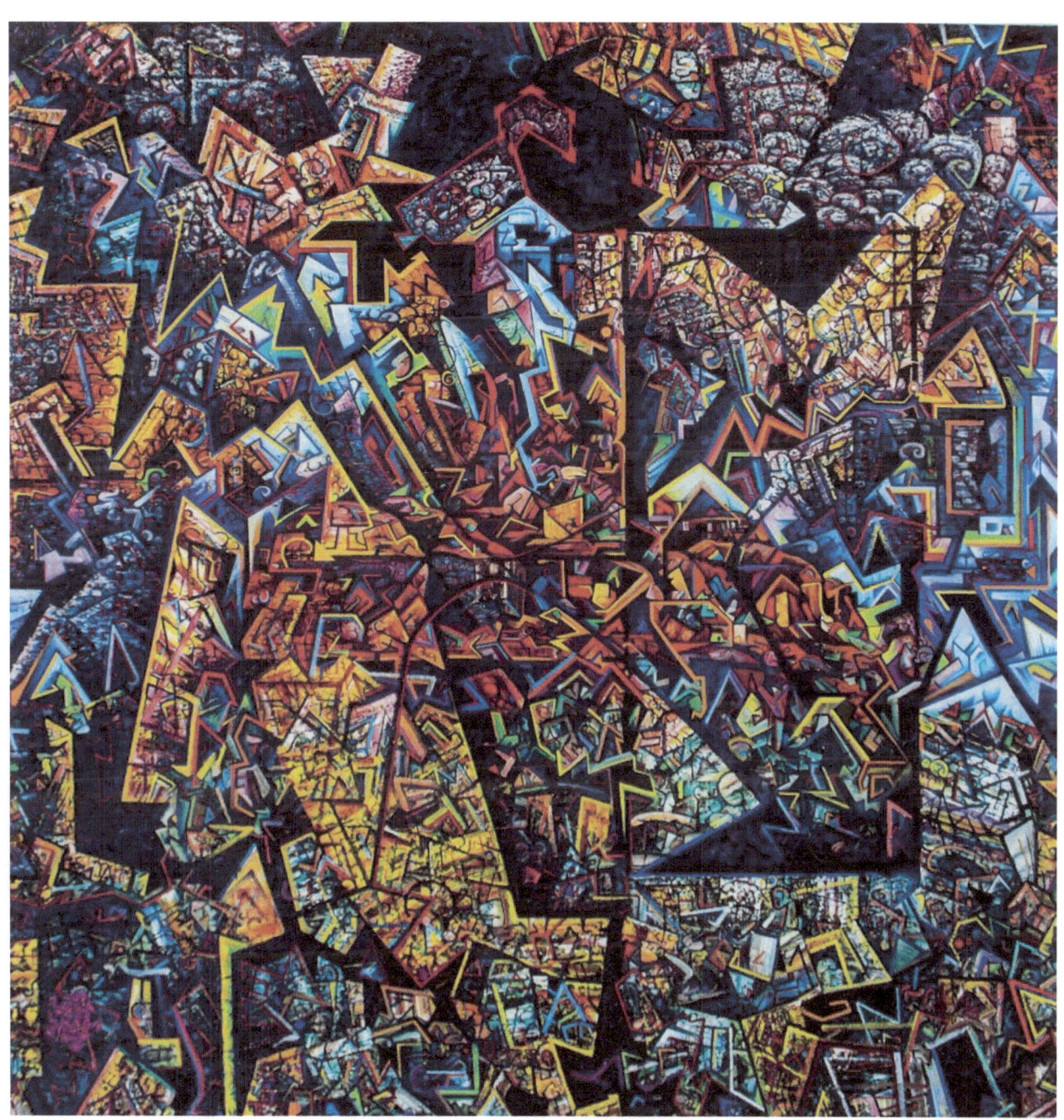

TOWARD THE TORTOLITAS

1995 - 2013
Oil on Canvas
24" x 36"

We enact the game of "Hide and Seek" as we play in this landscape. There is a sweeping sense of cloud formations, saguaro, mountains and sun; all blown by invisible winds. Our eyes "find" a green cactus here, there a ray of golden sunrise and, improbably, the brilliant red of desert sunset. By the twin lights of sunrise and sunset, Vytas breaks trail for our trek toward the Tortolitas.

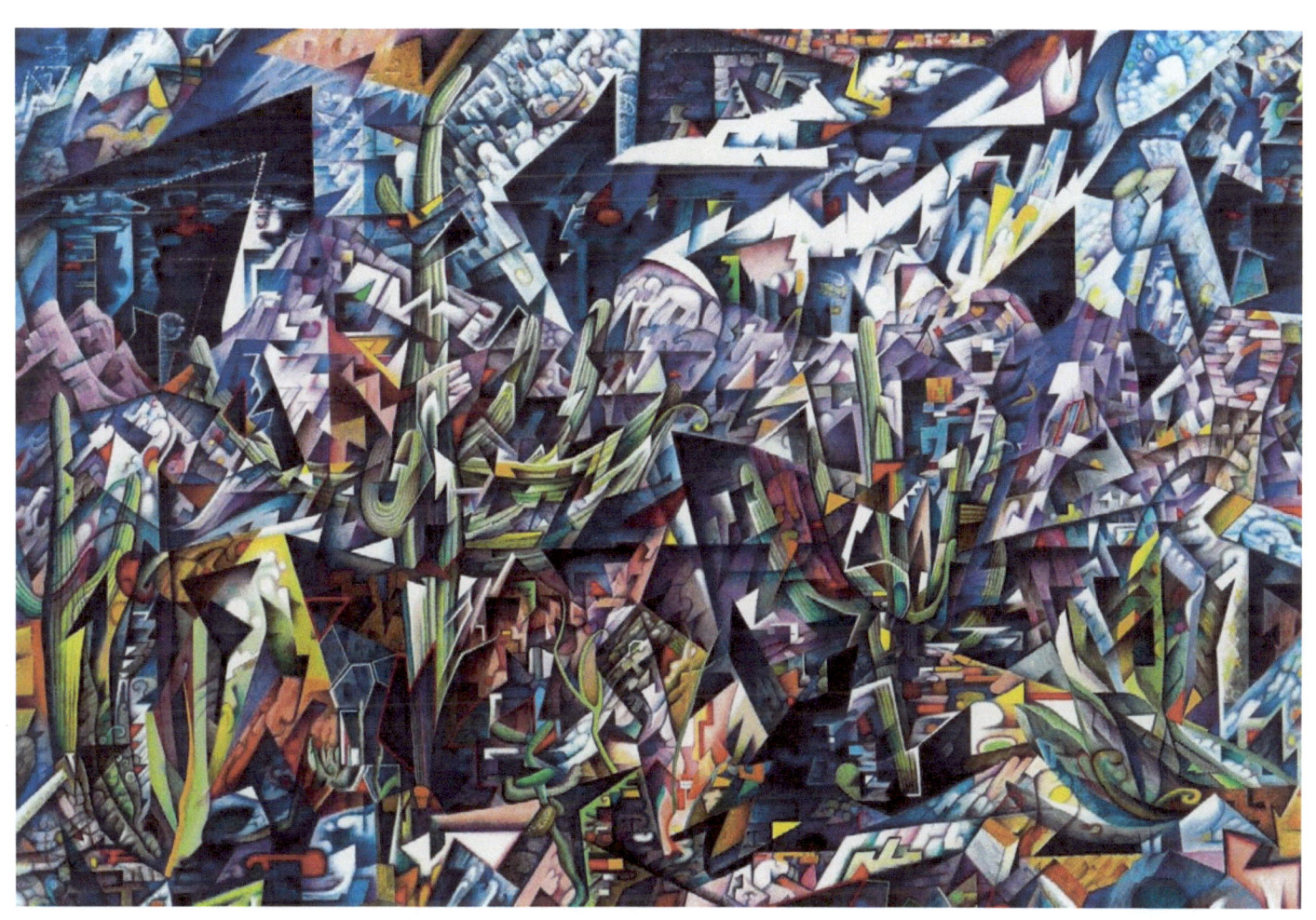

THE INNERNET

1985 - 2000
Oil on Canvas
96" x 108"

There is something about the dark that fascinates.
We are drawn inexorably to the shadows of others; those
parts that we see and they cannot. It is strange how the
unconscious, that old iceberg, is unknown to us. Try as
we might, that which is conscious, the iceberg tip, can
apprehend only what it knows. In this painting we can
see a tremendous amount of dark matter, negative space,
formlessness, unconsciousness...........whatever term we
want to apply. It makes us look for relief to the wonderful
objects that comprise the rest of the painting.

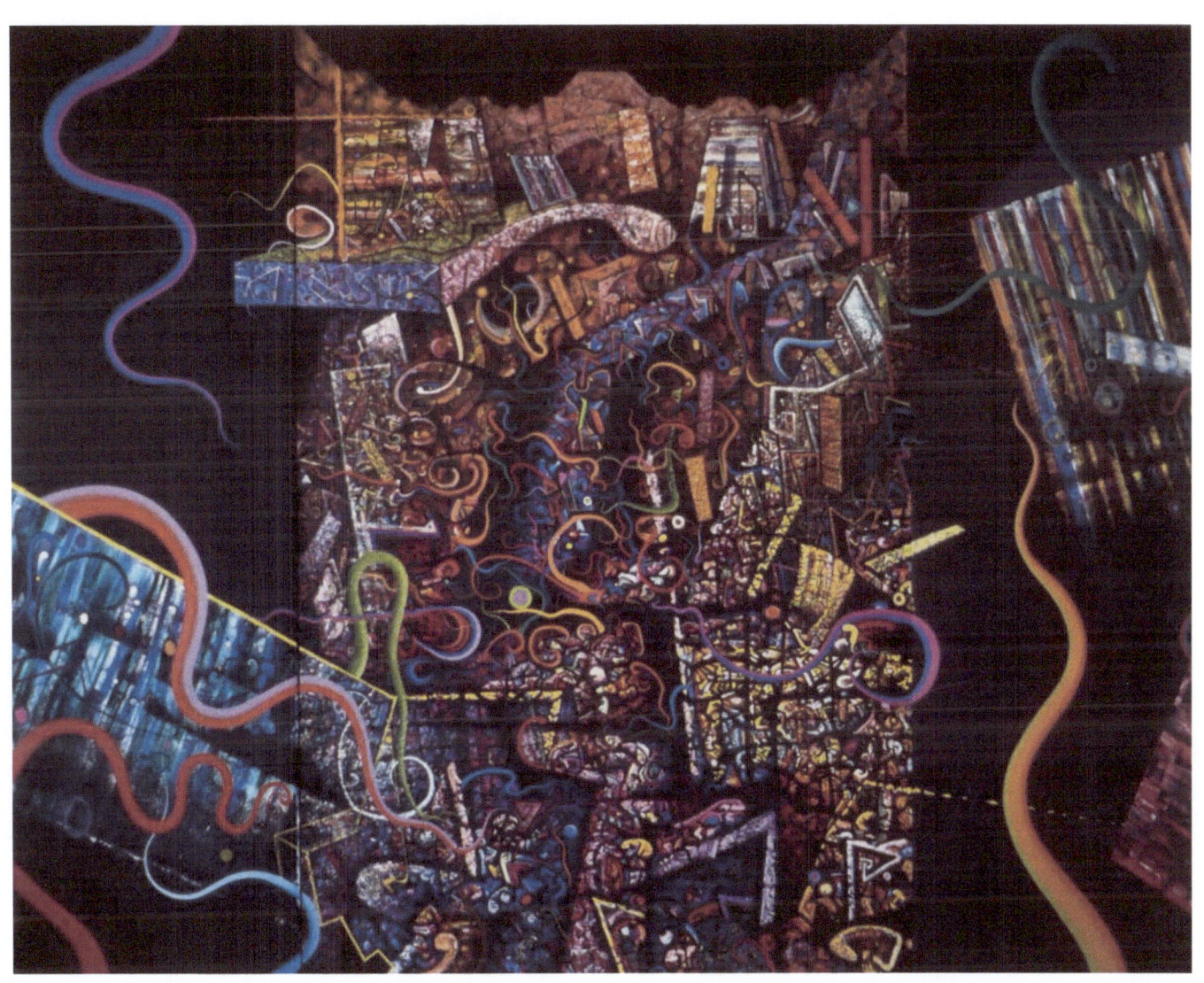

ATMANSPHERE 2

2001
Oil on Canvas
18" x 14"

These forms might be carefully folded thoughts residing in the brain. The blue lines slice through gray matter like brilliant ideas making grooves in memory. Memory and imagination play inside our minds creating a narrative of new meaning. There are spaces and lines here that are open to the architecture of communication between painting and viewer. After we look away, we find those spaces and lines are now memories in our brains. We take the painting with us.

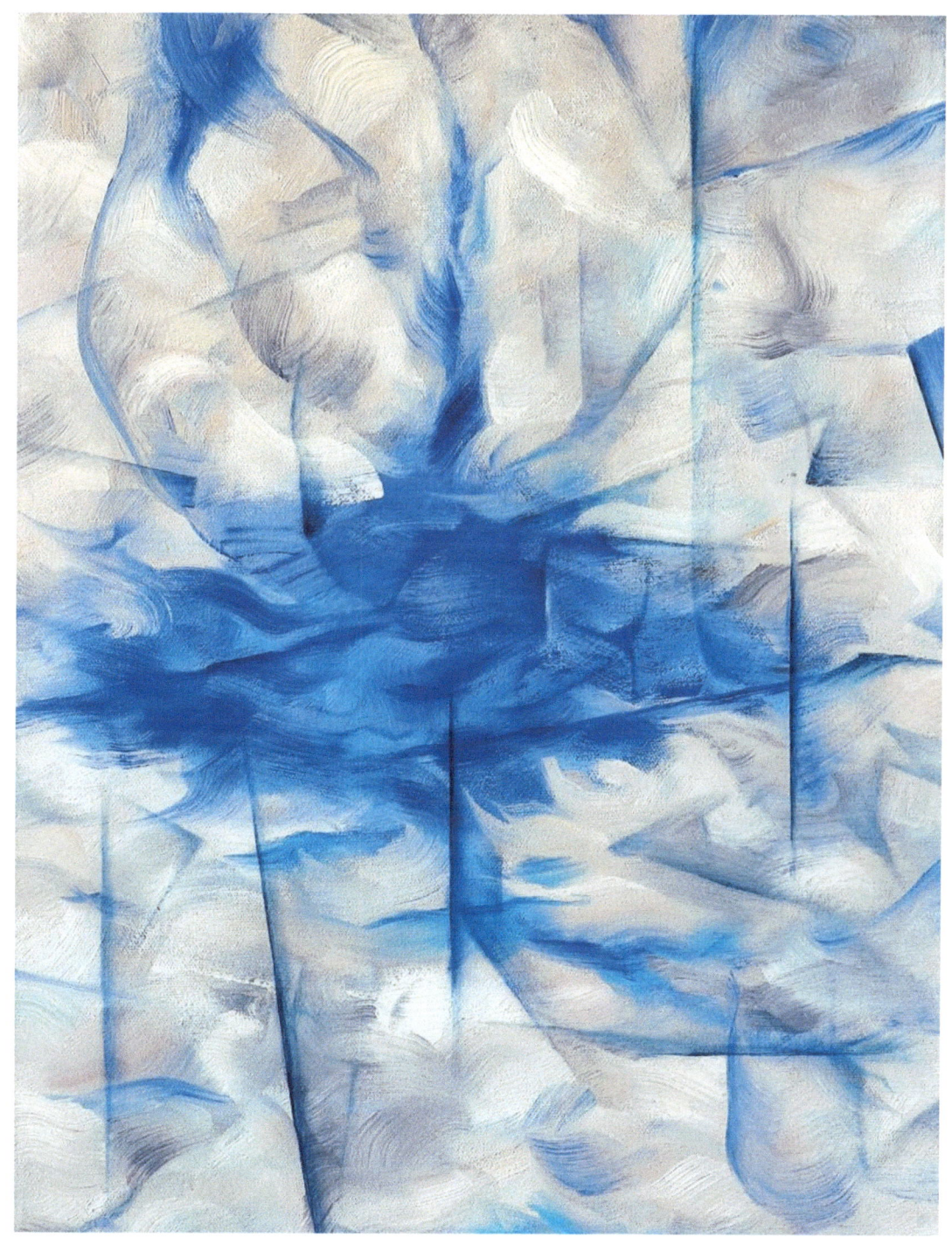

ATMANSPHERE 6

2004 - 2017
Oil on Canvas
18" x 14"

There are discernible shapes that look like they were fashioned in order to juxtapose the sense of fluid movement with the fixed and immobile. It creates tension, strengthening a sense of shattering. We feel like something has broken open and we can see the substrate of an object that once lived. It is like searching into an archeological dig and finding an artifact built from something organic. The colors speak of mythic Atlantis and other imagined treasures that come from the ocean. This could have been a piece of Neptune's trident or part of a ship that sailed on forgotten seas.

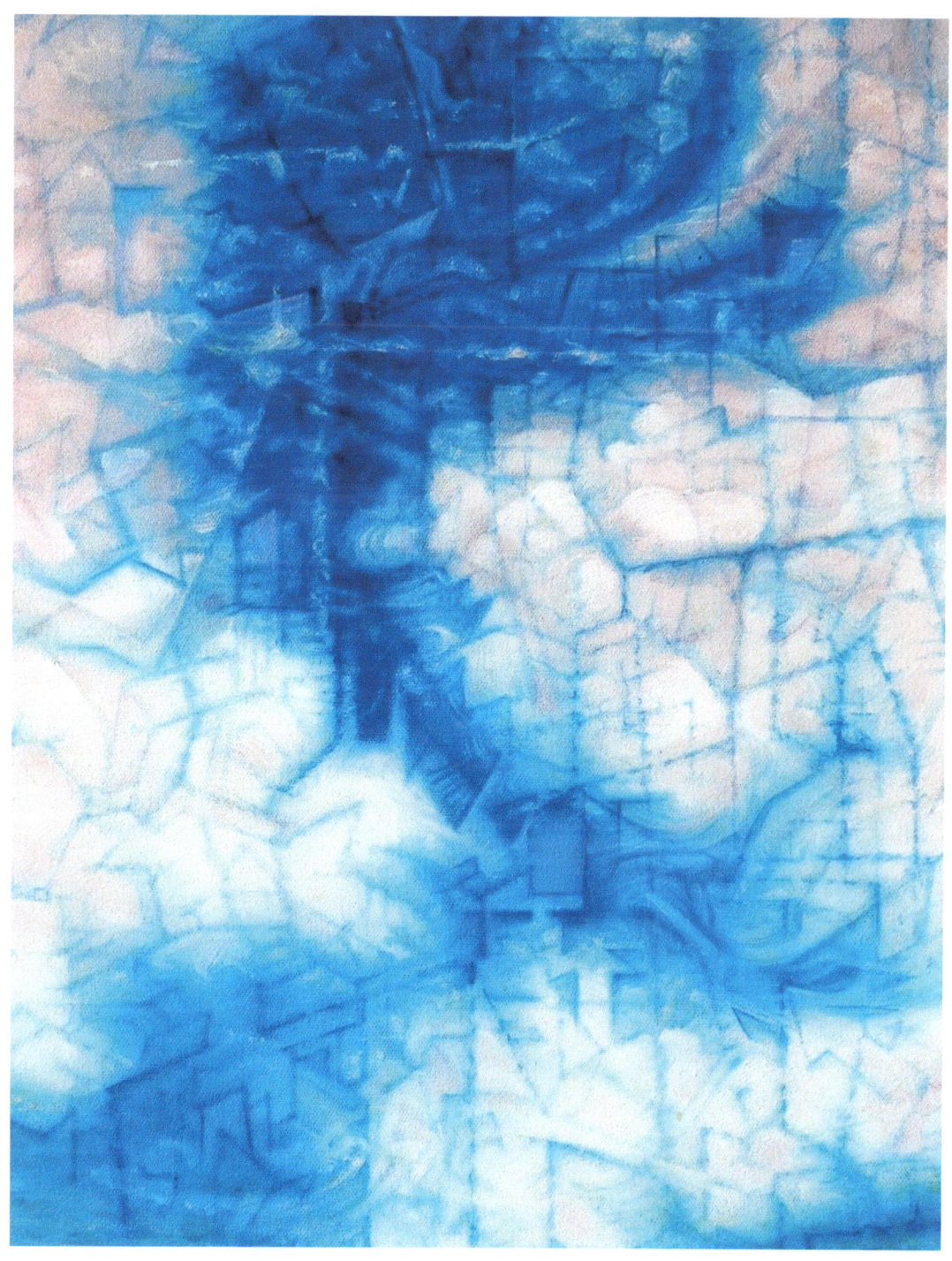

ATMANSPHERE 7

2001 - 2010
Oil on Canvas
48" x 60"

Atman refers to an individual self. That individual self yearns for the realization of the true self, Brahman. This painting reminds us of the twists and turns the self experiences on its journey to break through the confines of ego-bound self and enter into the reality of Brahman. There are myriad distractions; beautiful forms, shapes, colors, by-paths and roads that can detain us from our quest. All the phenomena the artist has composed for us here still point to that which is ineffable and invisible, the bliss of transcendent self.

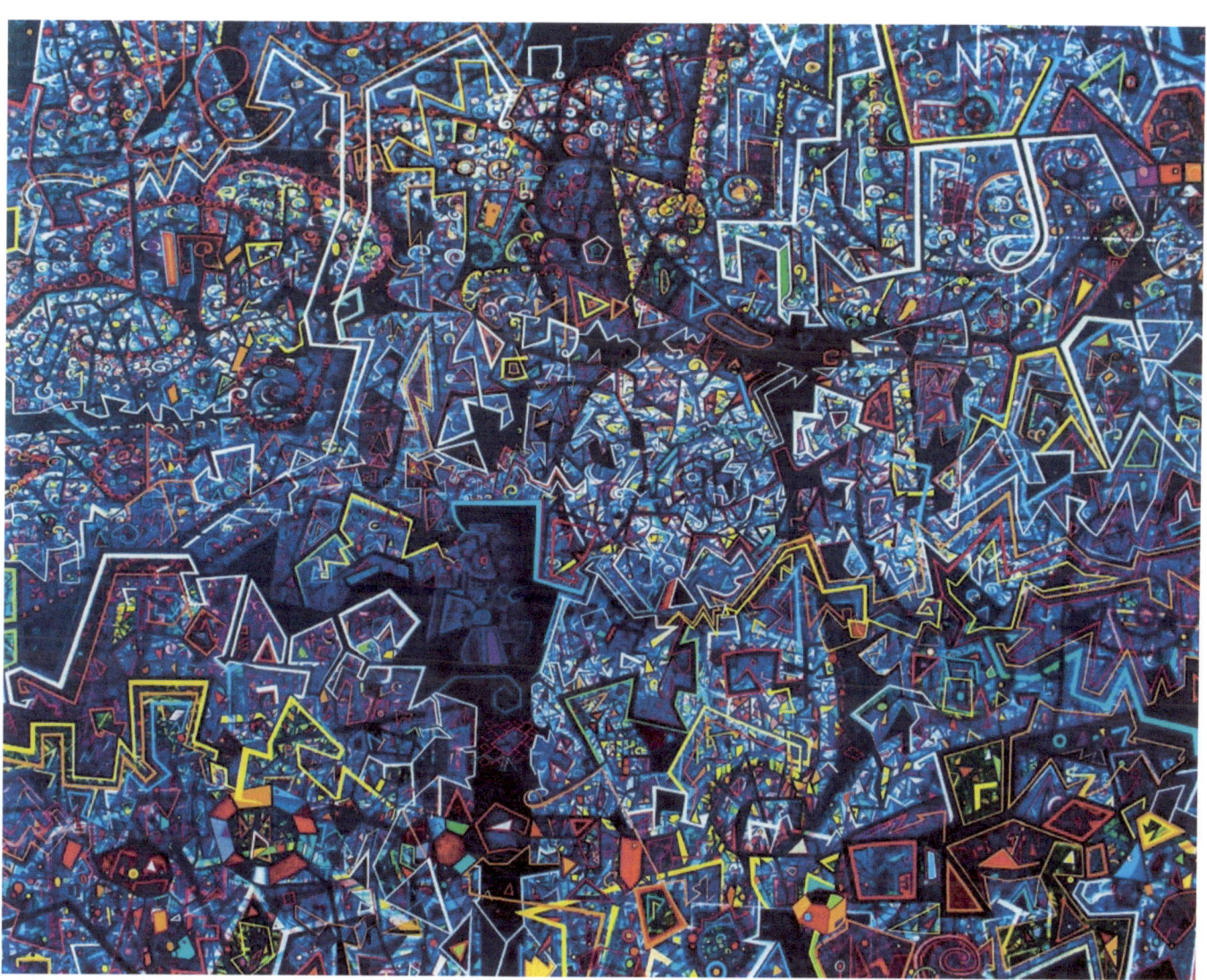

ATMANSPHERE 10
(POST-ORGASMIC BLISS)

2002 - 2004
Oil on Canvas
48" x 60"

We are able to witness the aftermath of passion; sperm cells, ova, planets and starbursts. All these phenomena represent a way of back-mapping to our own conception when we left the realm of bliss and unknowing and entered the world of sound and light. There is wonderful radiance in this work. It is like light itself is the source of life and the bright intertwining of colorful tendrils speak of the passionate love affair between the artist and his work.

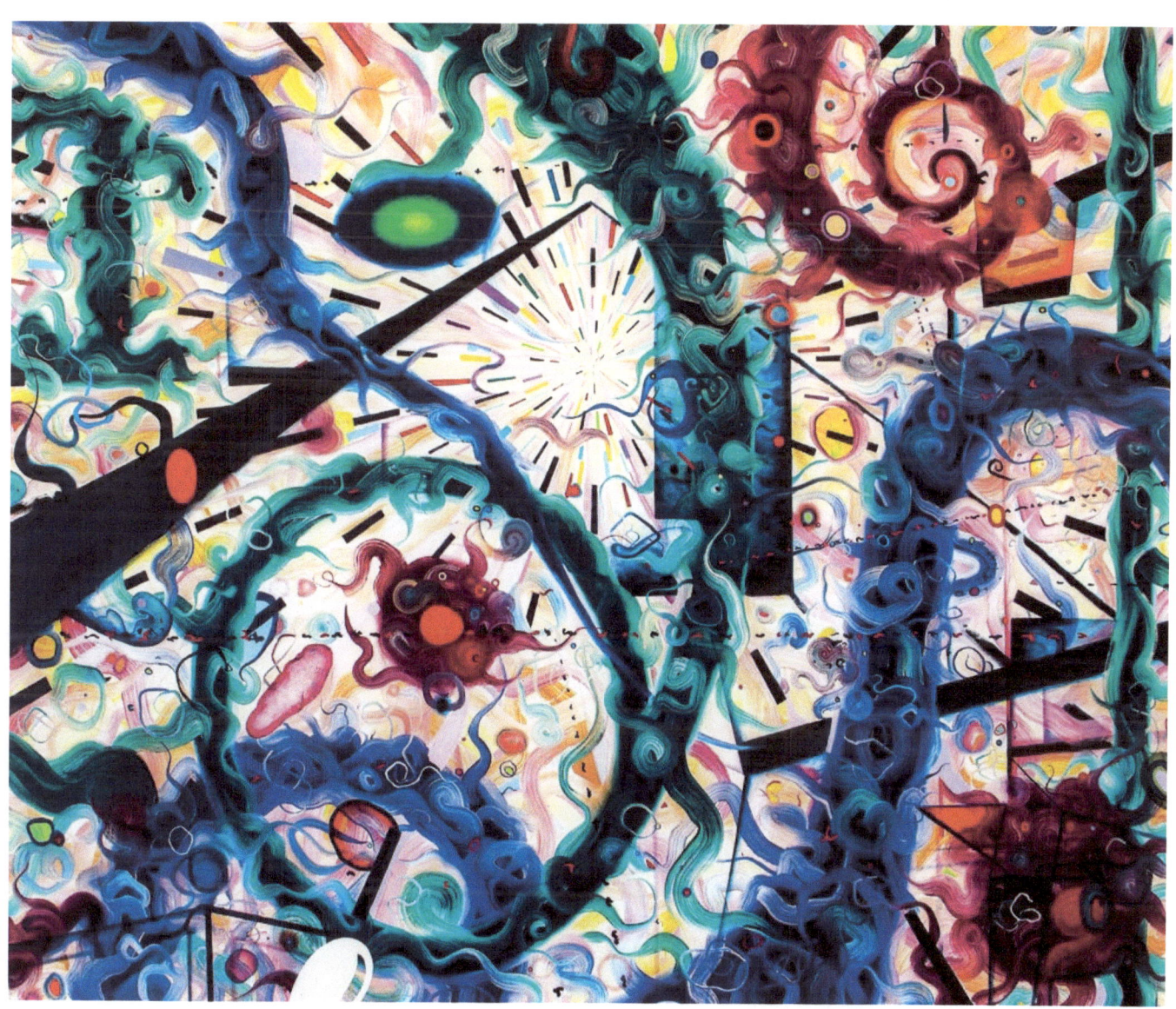

ATMANSPHERE 12

2002
Oil on Canvas
48" x 60"

At first glance, this might be seen as rain water splashed on a glass window. If we look closely, tiny lines seem to define the longitude and latitude of an enormous reach. Maybe this is an architectural schematic of the ocean or a way to comprehend the dark matter of space. There is mystery in this message. It is a map helping us find our bearings in a new place.

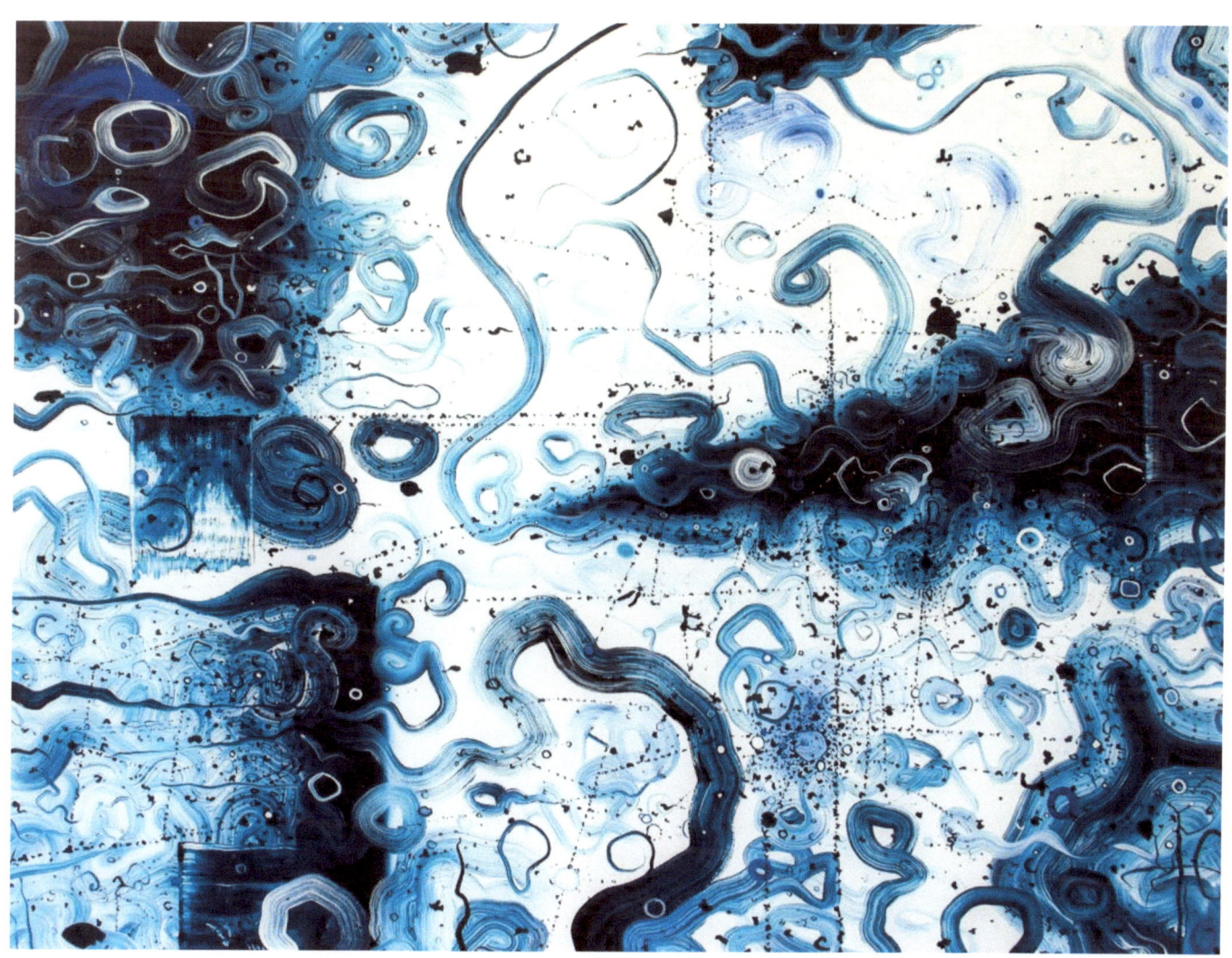

ATMANSPHERE 13

2002 - 2014
Oil on Canvas
48" x 36"

Twelve years live upon the canvas as planets, solar systems and what might be an introduction to our own self-witnessing. Beyond embryonic, this seems like we are transported a great distance into space; we have a view from afar. The mind embraces the vista and yearns to make contact with the work. There, within all that phenomena, appears an intelligent eye that meets our distant gaze and recognizes itself. We arrive from our journey to a place of identity. Vytas has provided us safe passage for self discovery.

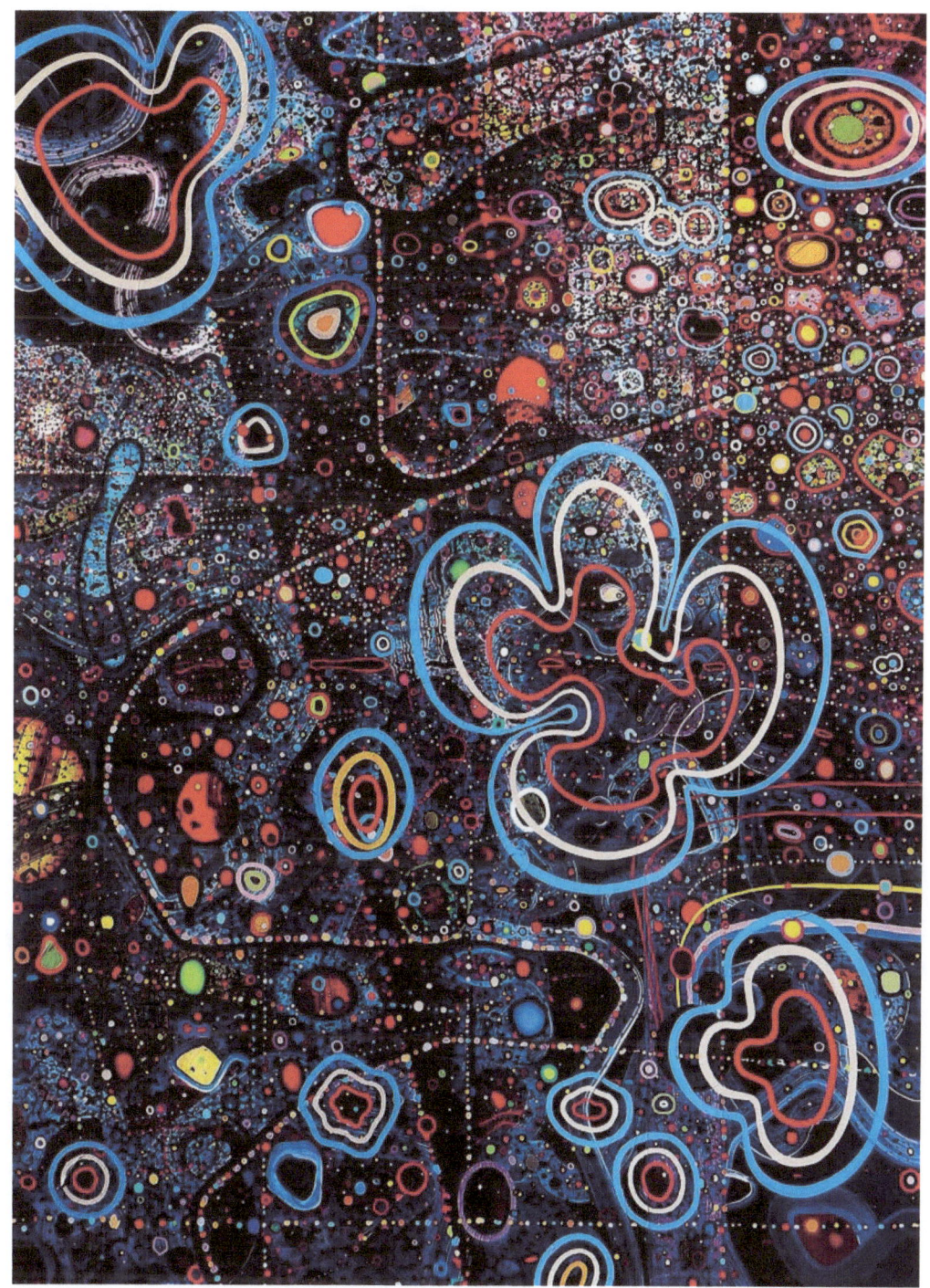

ATMANSPHERE 15

2002 – 2011
Oil on Canvas
60" x 48"
Collection of the Lewben Art Foundation
Vilnius, Lithuania

Ah, the sensuality of the curvilinear. There are curves within curves, circles embedded in arced forms, and color. The use of bright color on earth-toned shapes gives rise to a splendid sense of being grounded and yet that ground is fixed upon the dark of space. Vytas does not allow us to rest. His exploration of inner and outer space engenders a gypsy desire, deep inside our vagabond hearts, to roam with him across the universe of his mind.

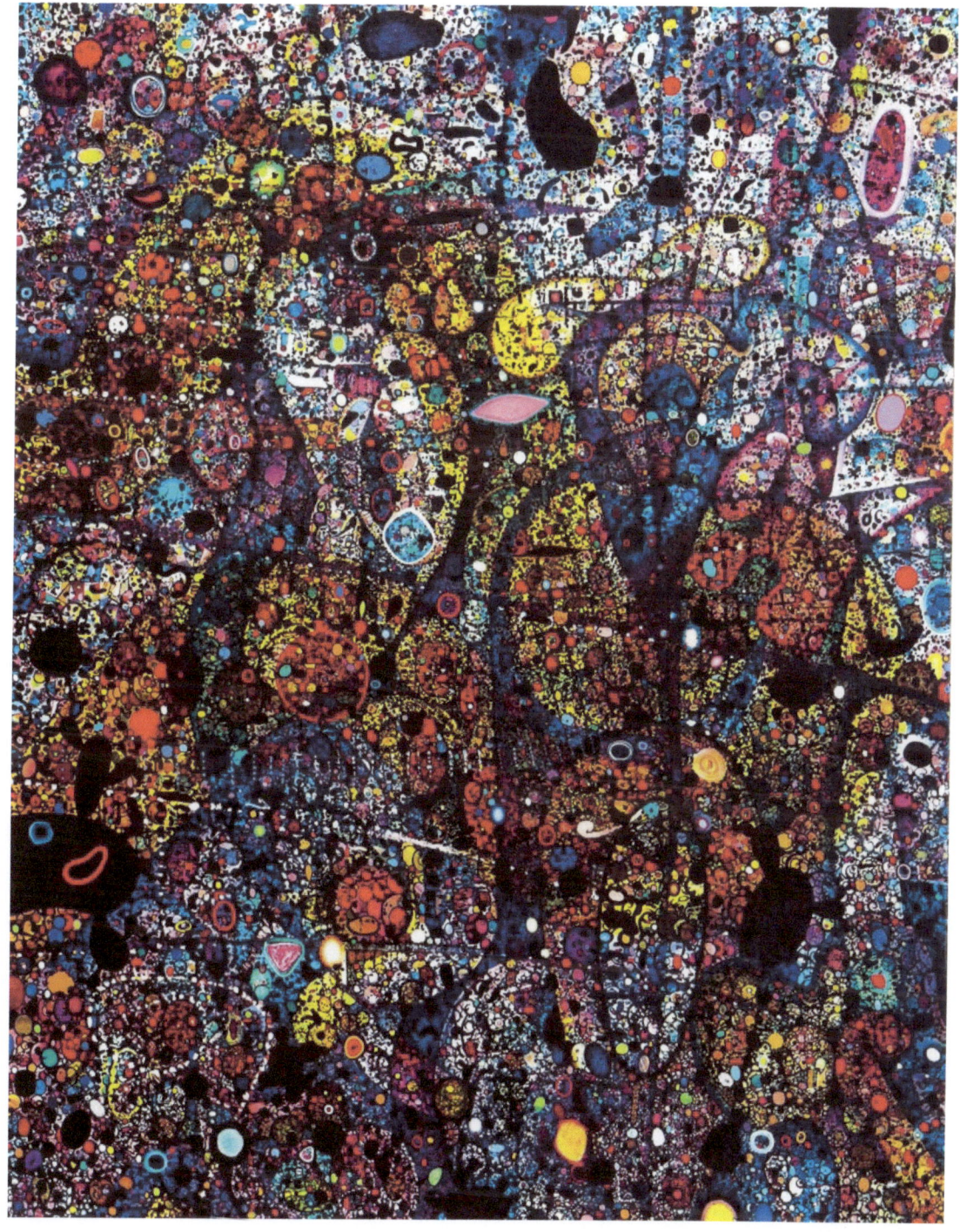

ATMANSPHERE 17
VERSION 5

2004 - 2016
Oil on Canvas
48" x 60"

This painting is alive. The energy that sends planets whirling around the sun, that burns deep within all the suns and stars, is burning inside this magical field. Vytas has captured the fire that first touched the deep and brought life into being; the generative flame of creation. Here, life forms begin to emerge within a context of great balance and beauty. Nothing needs to be added or removed. It is all here, full and resplendent.

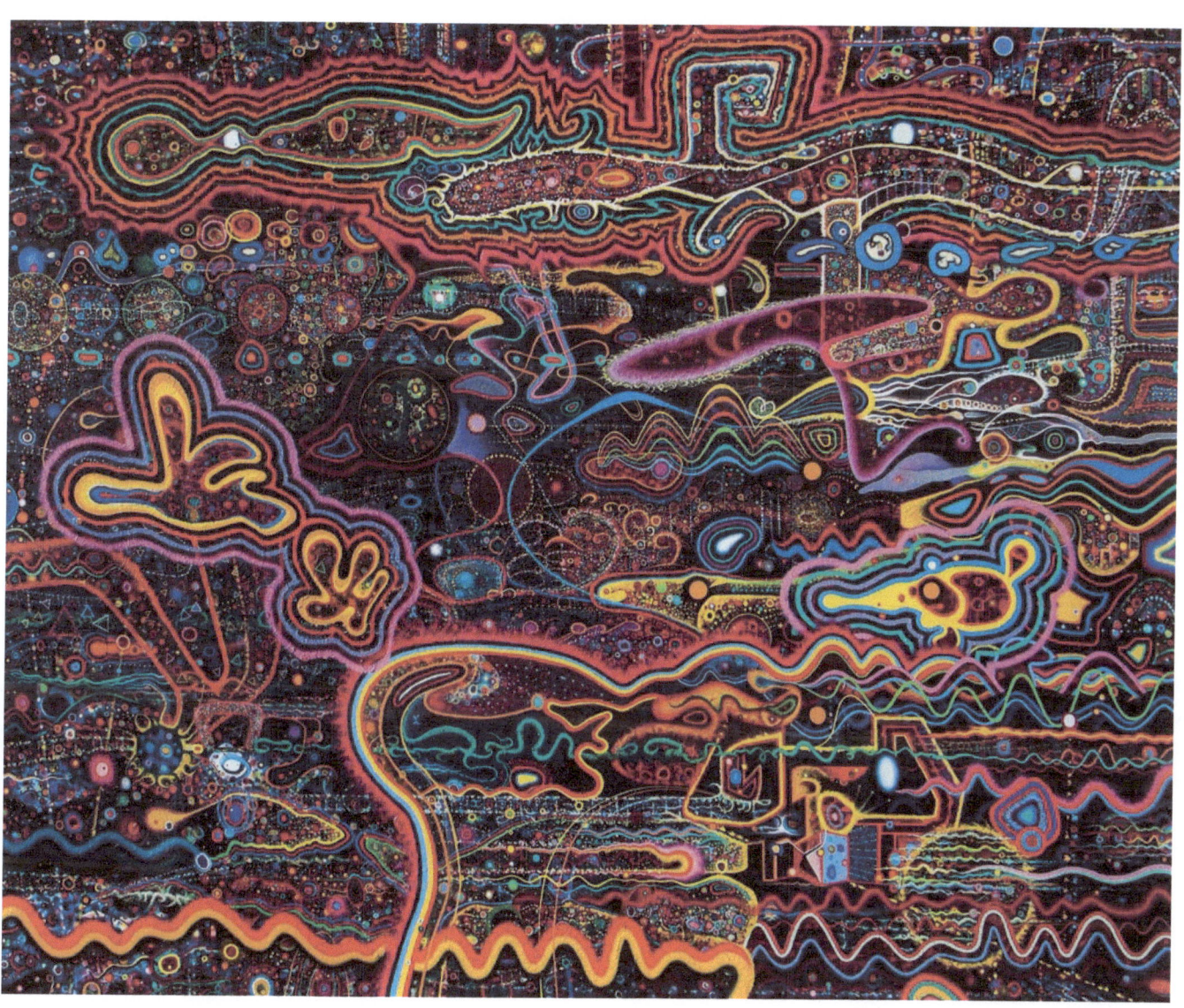

ATMANSPHERE 18

2004 - 2013
Oil on Canvas
48″ x 60″

This is a schematic of nine years of vision. It appears
alive, as if the individual elements are corpuscles and
plasma of something immense. Perhaps the weight of
light encompasses cells like these. They move, coalesce,
and speak of a sentience embedded in each gloriously
radiant part, the meaning of which is revealed deep
inside our own life stream.

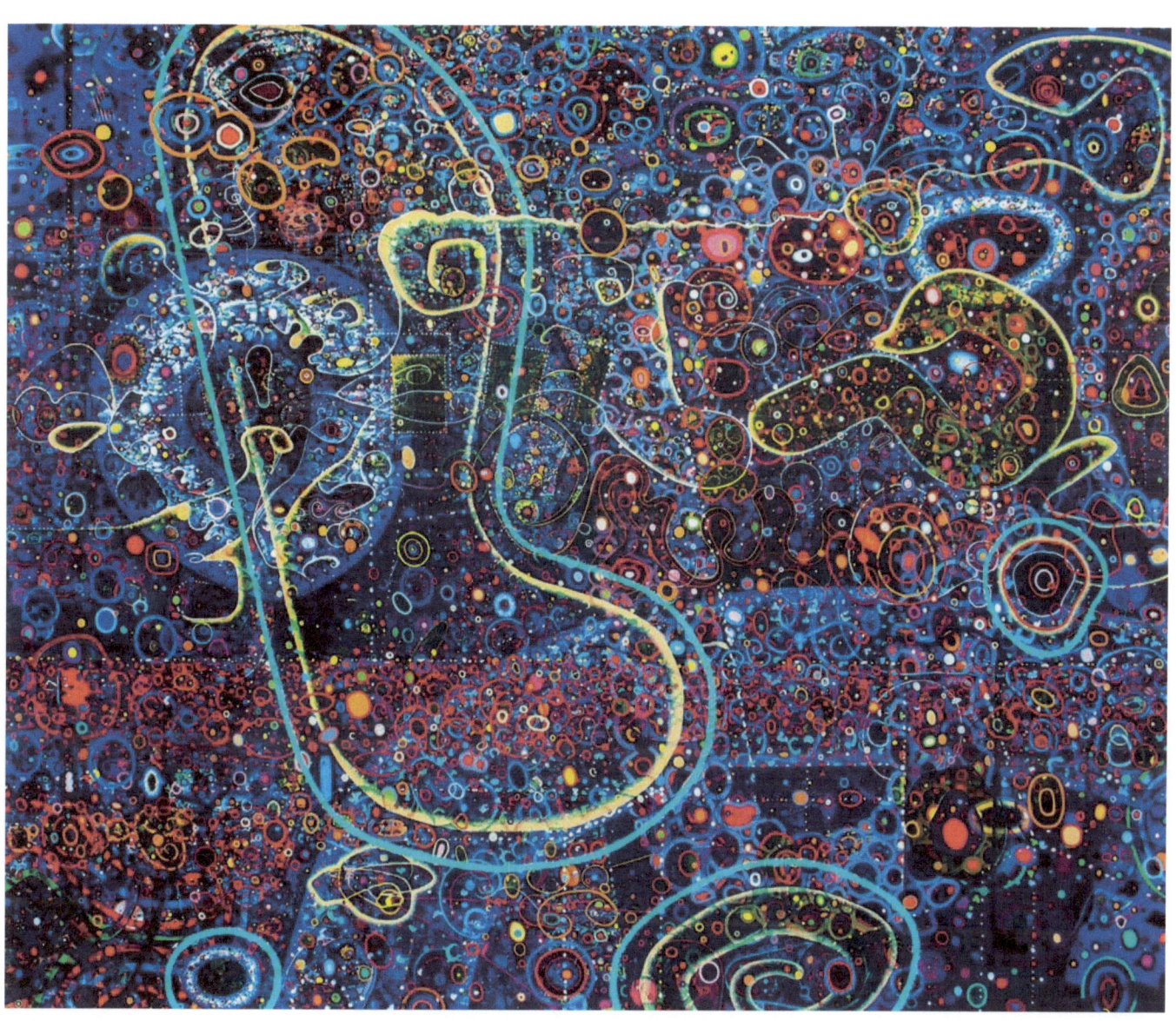

ATMANSPHERE 19
VERSION 2

2004 - 2016
Oil on Canvas
48" x 36"

This painting locks our gaze. We are unable to deal with it in pieces; we must see the Gestalt. The pieces are like a kaleidoscope that has a fixed pattern and yet there are no similar pieces within that whole. It is rather like life. We try to take a bit of it at a time and cannot. It is all there, all around us, at every place, time and space. The turquoise keeps drawing us to it as though it is a special key we use for unlocking the secrets hidden in these shapes. We follow the turquoise path searching for the lock. That is the secret. We are able to enter this painting because it is the lock and our eyes are the key.

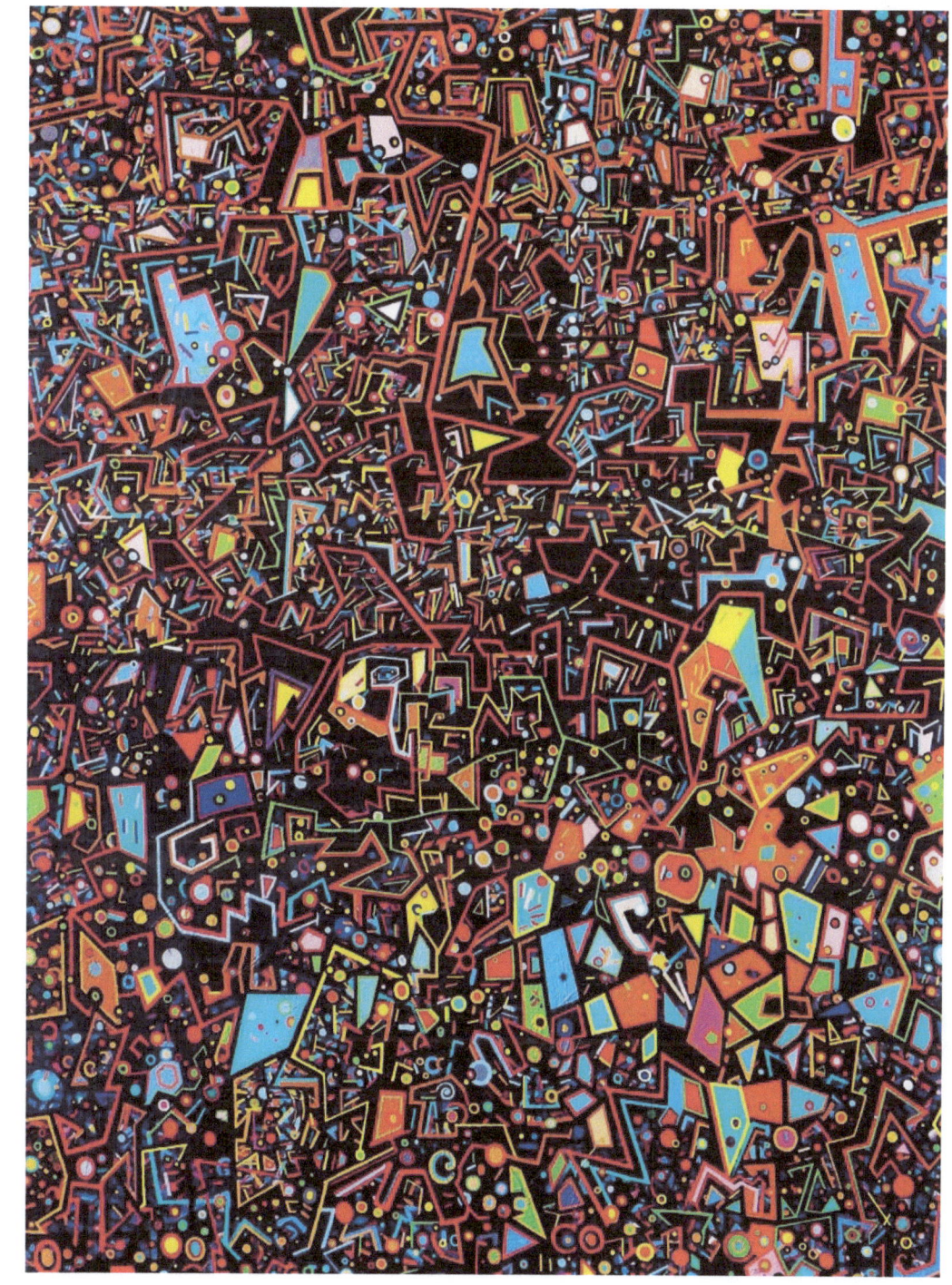

ATMANSPHERE 22

2005
Oil over acrylic on canvas
60" x 48"

This painting is a battlefield against the enemy of impermanence. Vytas has filled the canvas with forms and structures that appear to have life. These highly organic shapes hold our eyes, guarding against the passage of time. Each form is placed with certainty as an anchor holding us within the confines of the frame. We feel safe in the vibrant color and the play of soft forms. We can come back to it again and again and it will be the same, a haven where we reside for a moment in wonder.

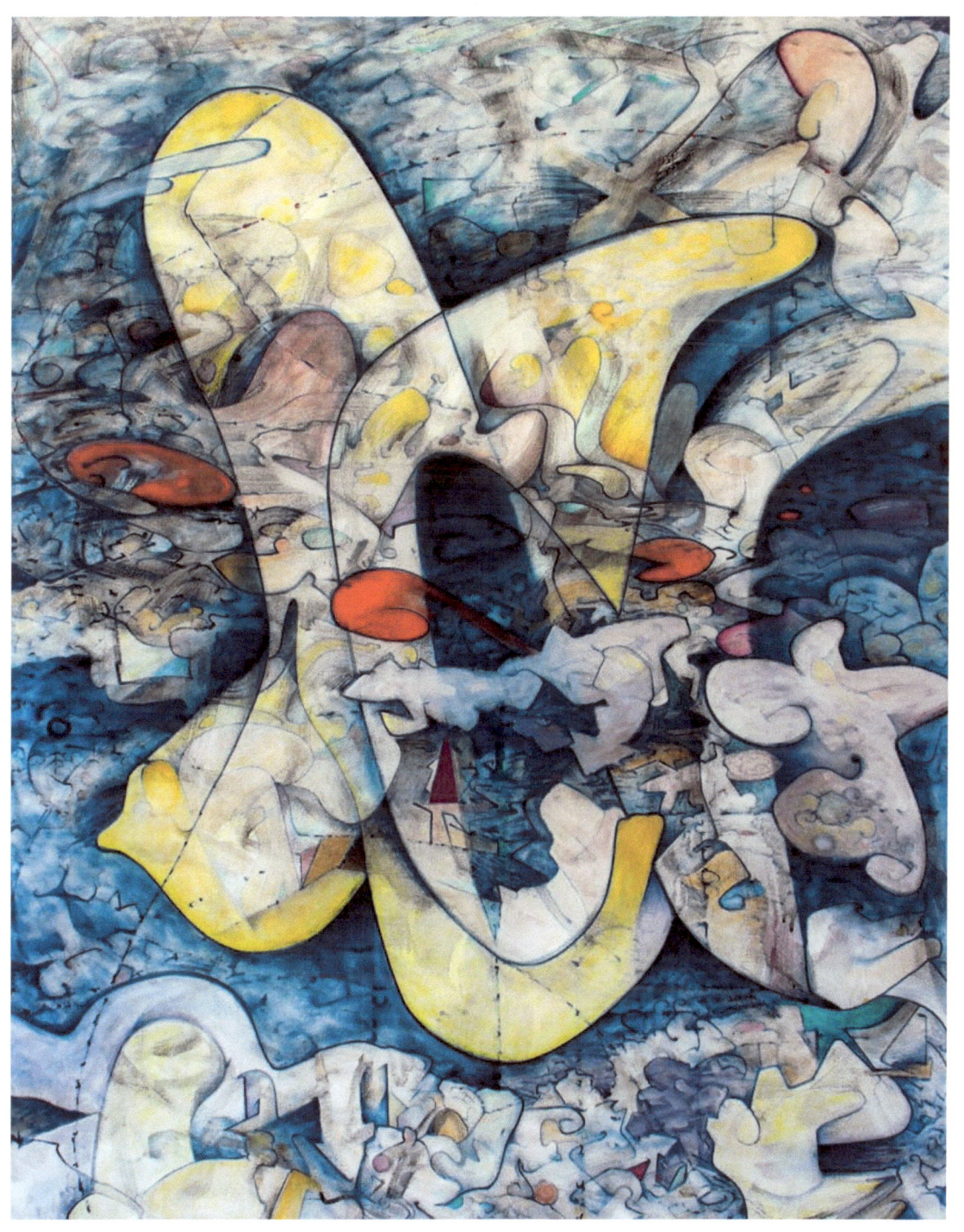

ATMANSPHERE 23

2005 - 2010
Oil over Acrylic on Canvas
48" x 60"
Collection of the Lewben Art Foundation
Vilnius, Lithuania

What secrets lie inside this strange landscape? There are dark areas in this piece, more than in most of Vytas' work. Sensuality permeates the entire canvas, dark and light areas alike, and we are drawn to places where they touch. Our eyes skirt along the edges of forms as though they are fingers, feeling far more than paint on canvas.

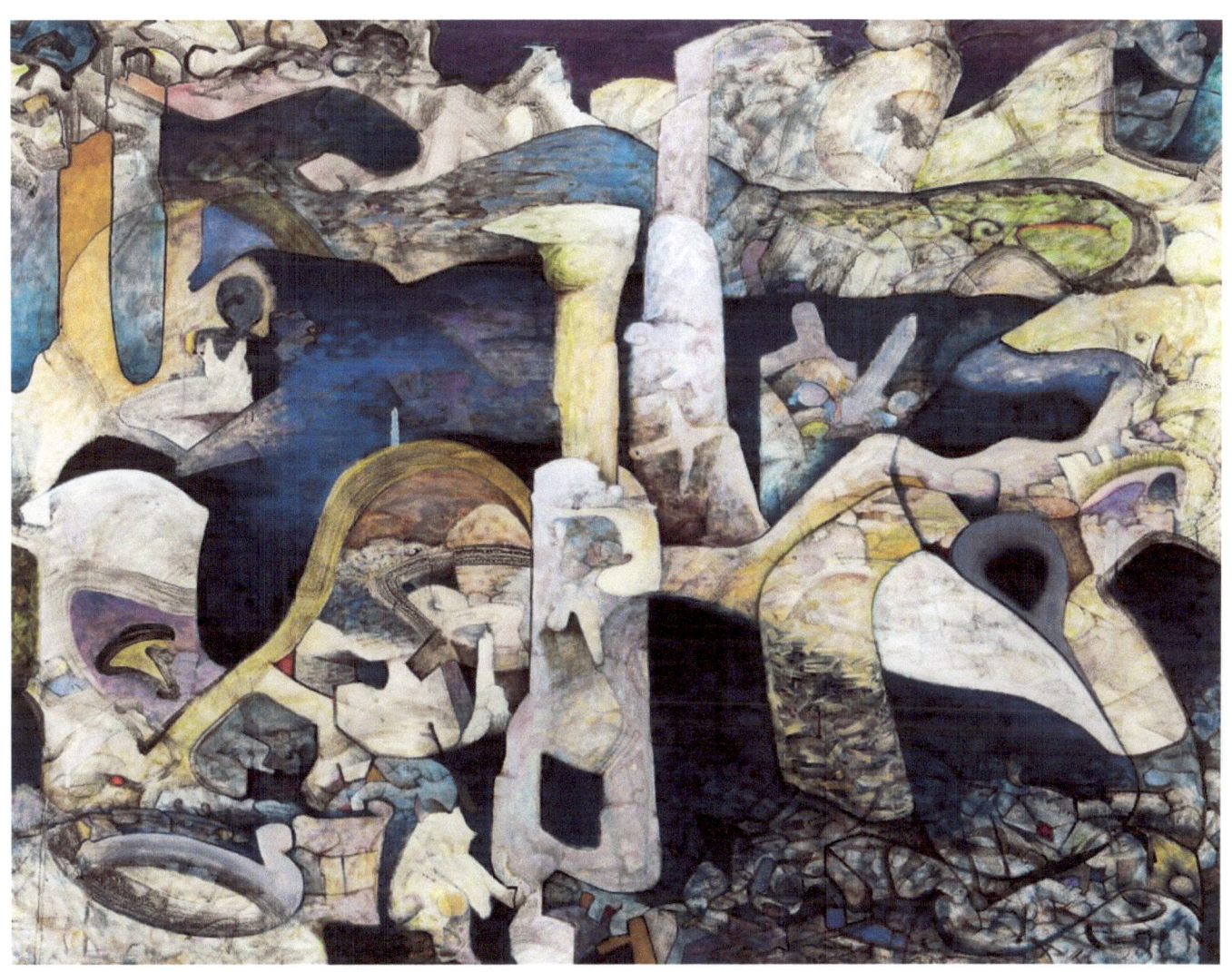

ATMANSPHERE 24

2005 - 2008
Oil over Acrylic on Canvas
48" x 60"

A celestial river has left treasure for us. Rocks, tumbled through time, shine from the depths of unseen water, their edges rounded and smooth. What great fortune for us to be here at the river's edge, panning for gold. We can take these treasures with us, hold them fast in memory and when we close our eyes, we might hear the sound of invisible water flowing through our lives.

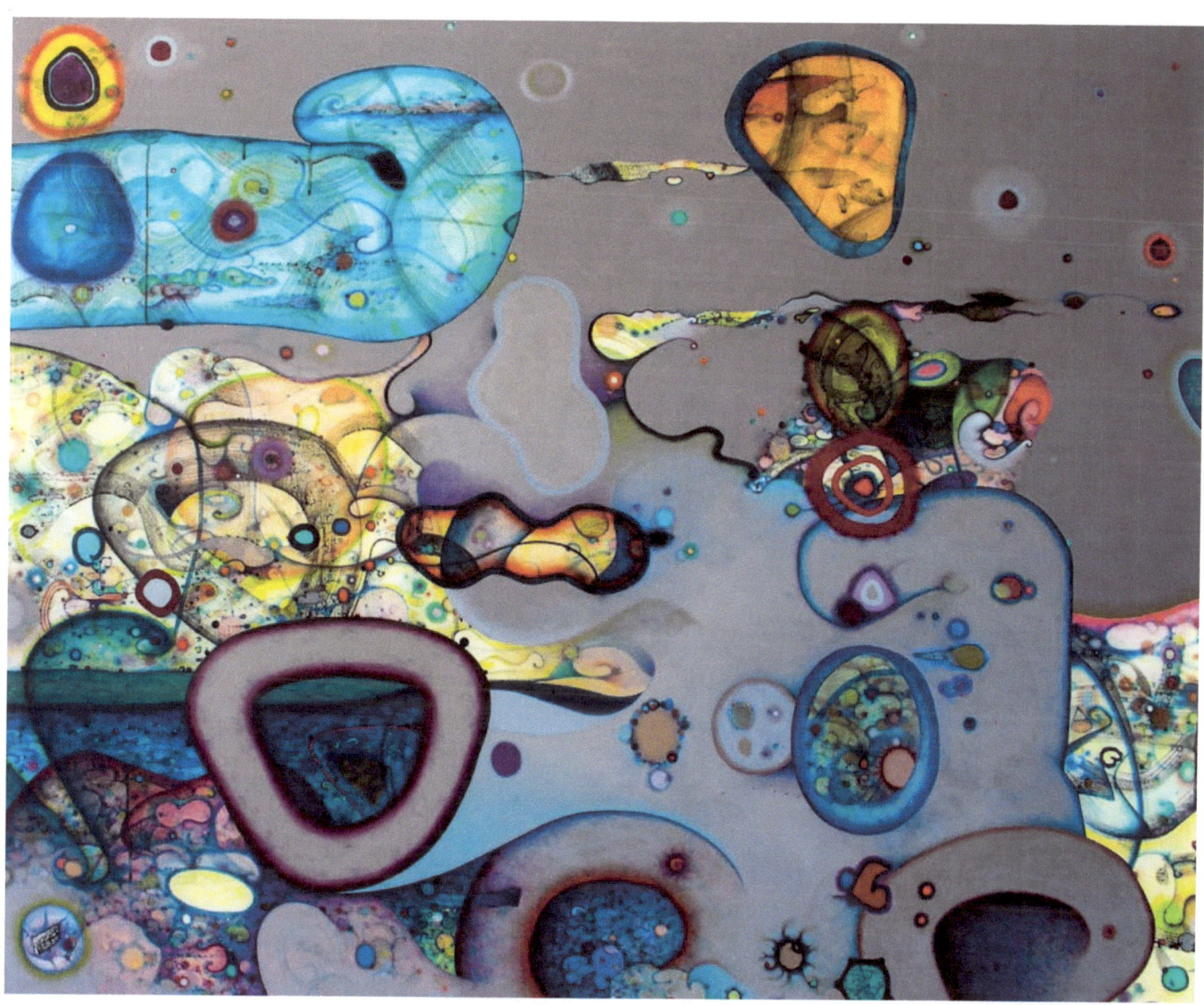

NIGHT CLOUD 11

2001
Oil on Canvas
60" x 48"

In deep night, lightning, laying bare the bones of the
sky, splinters the clouds. This lightning does not look as
though it is hotter than the surface of the sun and yet the
clouds show the paths cut by the strikes. The clouds are
moving, shattered by white fire. They will fall as rain,
broken, into the welcoming arms of the earth.

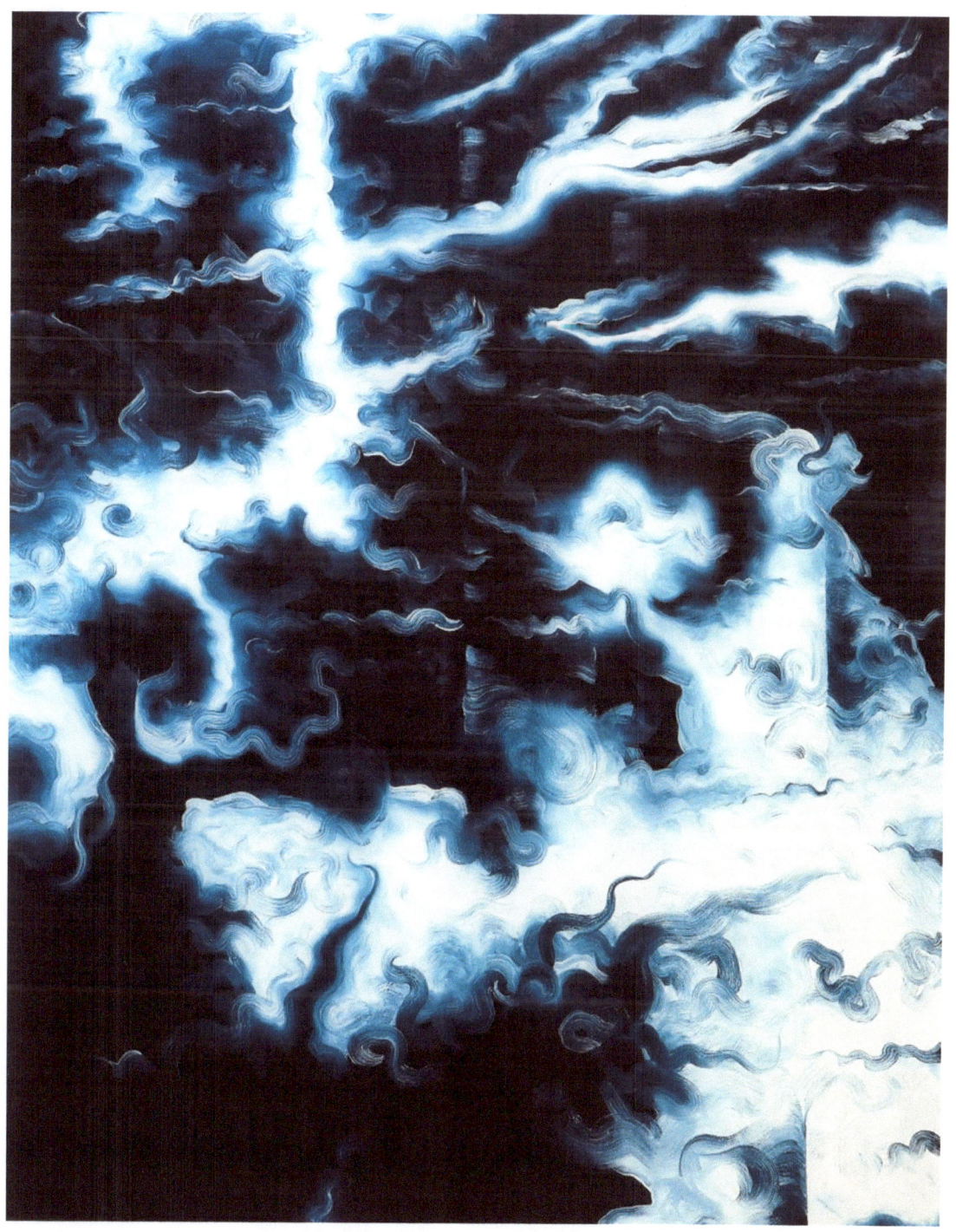

NIGHT CLOUD 14

2002 - 2004
Oil on canvas
48" x 60"

Here is the jagged dance of stars. Fragments of stellar dust
are magnified so we see the deep dance of light. Things
break. Promises, relationships, bones and hearts break.
Everything is impermanent. In this painting the shards
of what once existed pierce to the very blood of life. Each
piece has its own integrity but cannot connect, leaving
us with a feeling of immense distance, insurmountable
separation. The red drops are like pieces of the heart still
beating, still looking for union.

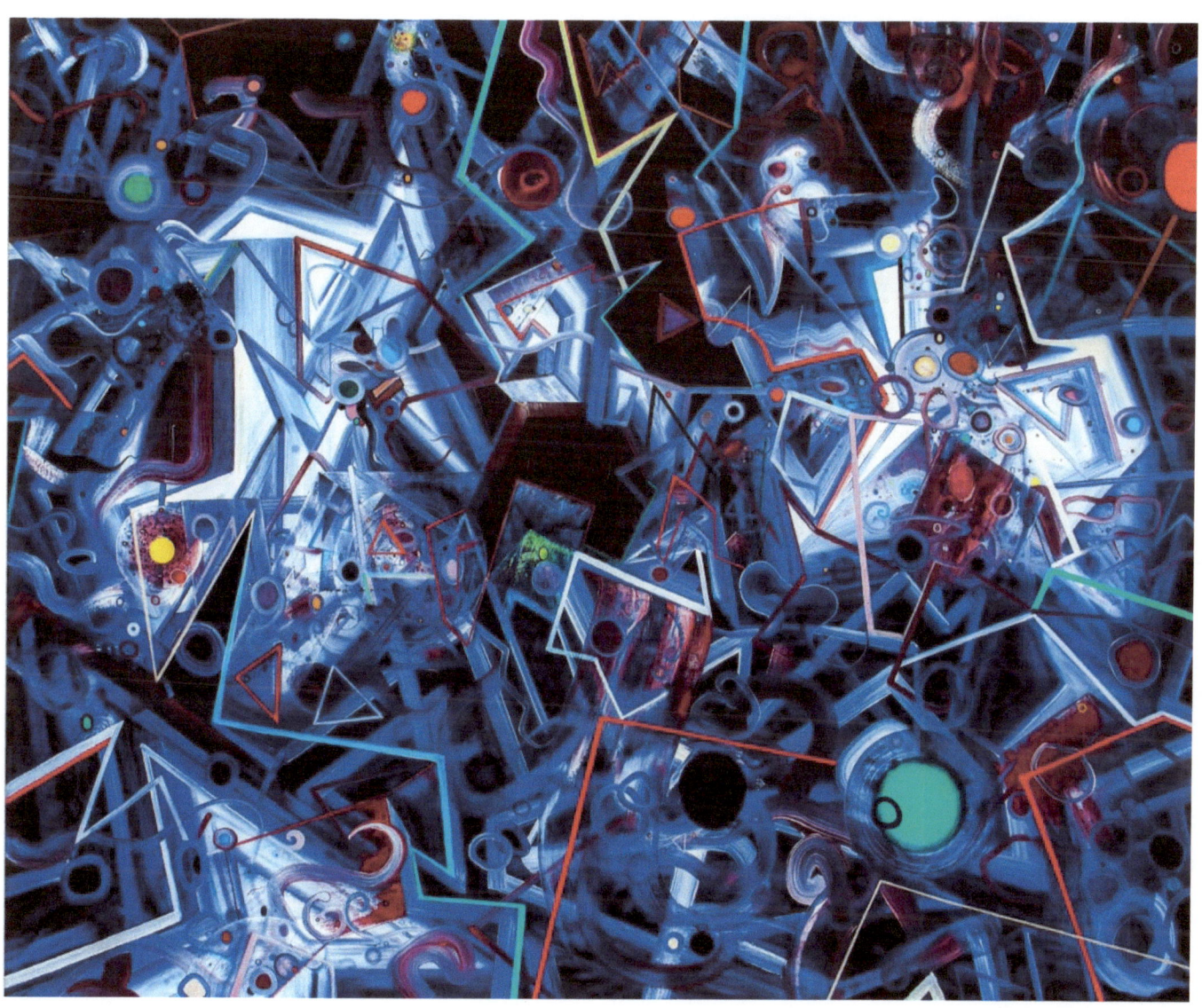

NIGHT CLOUD 20

2002
Oil on canvas
60" x 48"

The Southwest is home to Native myths and beings such as shape-shifters and ghost dancers. Vytas has conjured up hints of these beings and captured their essence. It looks as though this cloud is dancing across the sky. We might even imagine thunder sounding like the beat of rhythmic drums. When loved ones die, the Santa Clara Pueblo people say, "They went into the clouds". This cloud looks large enough to carry the prayers of all the living as they escort the dead back to their home in the sky.

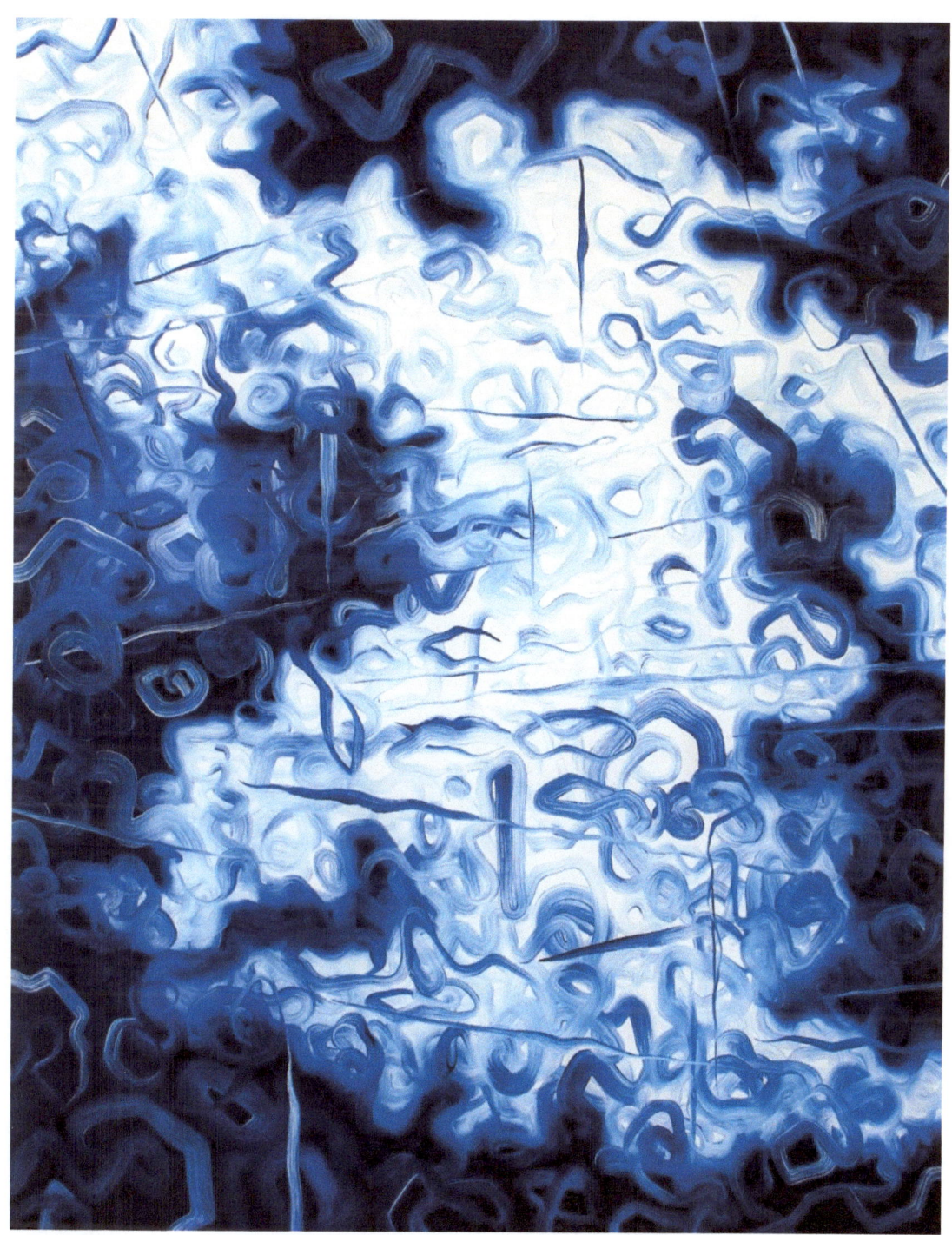

NIGHT CLOUD 22

2003 - 2004
Oil on Canvas
48" x 60"

Are these icy continents breaking apart in some ancient
ice age, in some primordial sea? Is this the water that gave
birth to life? The blue tones and fragmented pieces are
reminiscent of days when we cried. The salt brine tears
fell and where the drops landed, something started to
grow inside. Perhaps what grew was compassion for
self and others when we fully realized that we are not
alone in our suffering. We know that no matter when
we cry, there are others on this blue planet who are
crying with us.

-

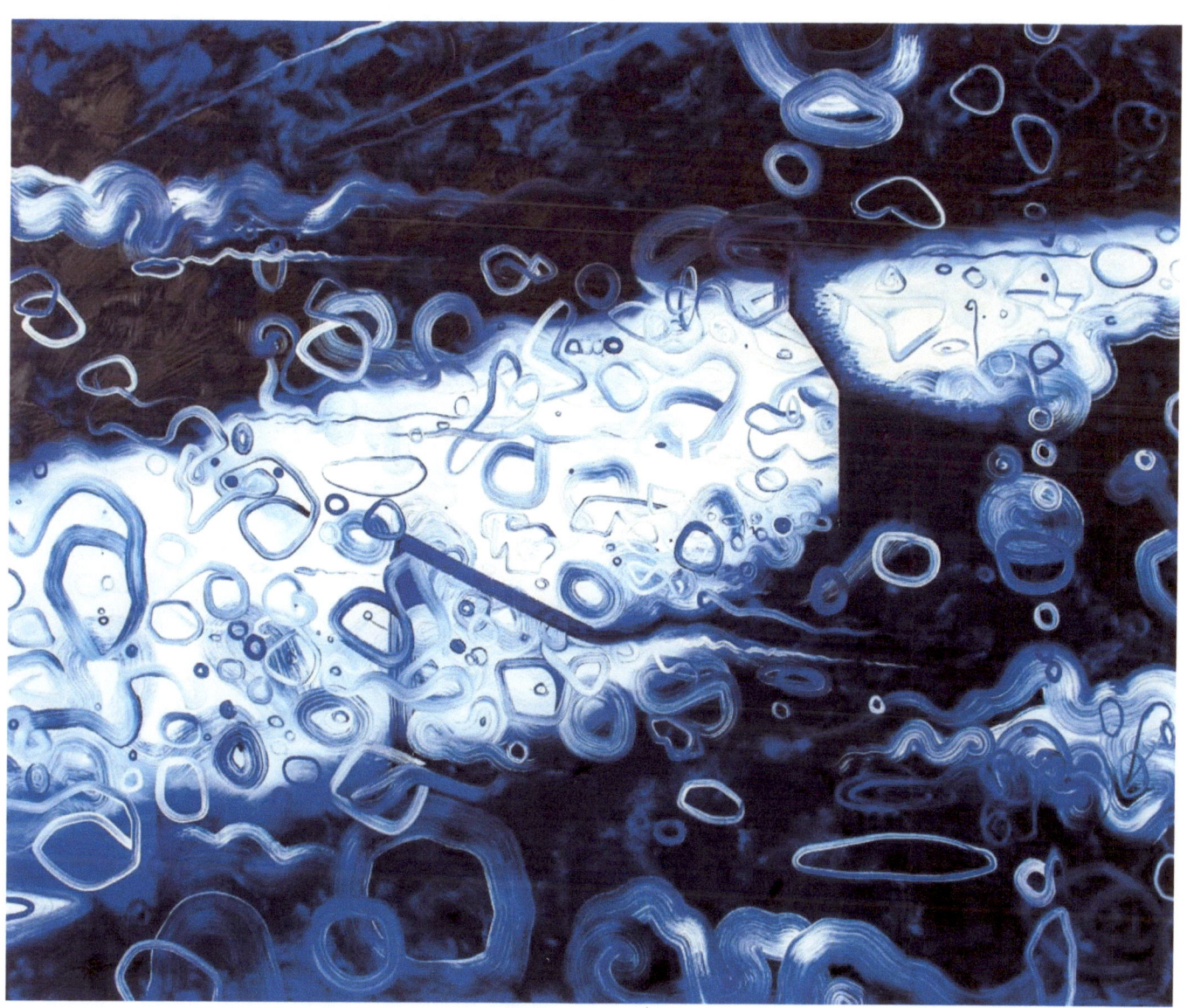

PLANETS

2005 - 2010
Oil over Acrylic on Canvas
60" x 48"
Collection of the Lewben Art Foundation
Vilnius, Lithuania

We humans search the night sky, read palms and gaze into crystal balls looking for clues everywhere, trying to understand our reality. Vytas is a map maker extraodinaire and as he transitions out of cubism, he plots the topography of a celestial destination, still leaving hints of where he has been. His focus on a segment of the cosmos calls us to adventure with him, to accompany him through this skyscape, to discover through his eyes, a place we've never been.

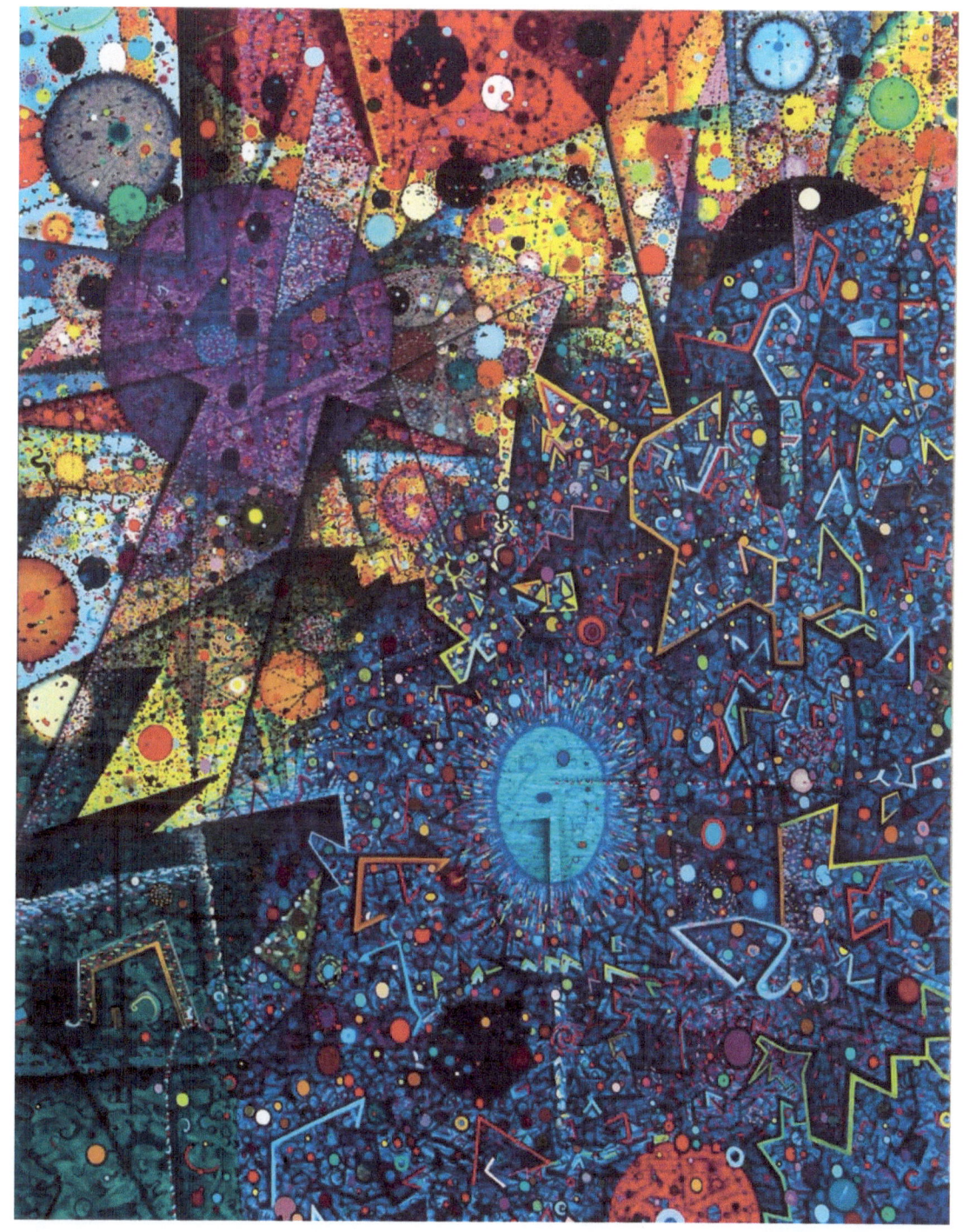

COLOR ANGEL

2006 - 2010
Oil on Canvas
48" x 60"
Collection of the Lewben Art Foundation
Vilnius, Lithuania

Vytas has broken light to reveal an angel inside. He stops its downward fall just where heaven and earth interface. We are unable to see this bright being in full circumference; the veil between the worlds occludes our view. We sense benevolence in the familiar colors of prismatic light and as the angel reaches out beyond the canvas, we are touched; caressed by a rainbow.

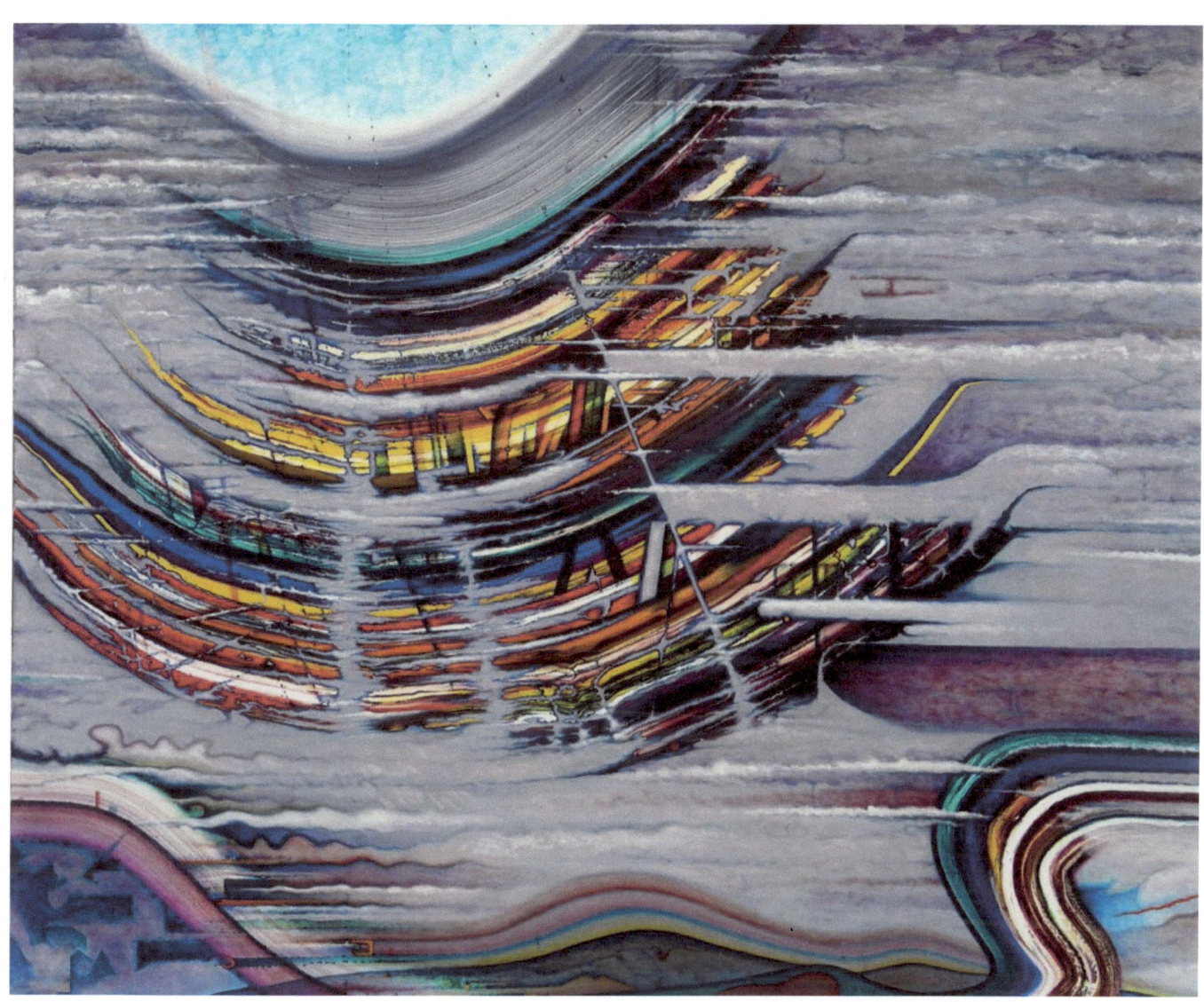

NODAL TRACES 4

2009 - 2014
Acrylic on Canvas
48" x 60"

Vytas has created depth and focus simultaneously. The curvilinear shapes dance with the linear while geometric rectangles frame individual scenes within this terrain. He captures our eye and we follow a path he has carefully plotted through a novel landscape. It's like riding in an invisible train where jeweled tracks lead us to fantastical places. There are windows, portals and places that call to us like the distant sound of someone calling our name just as we are falling asleep.

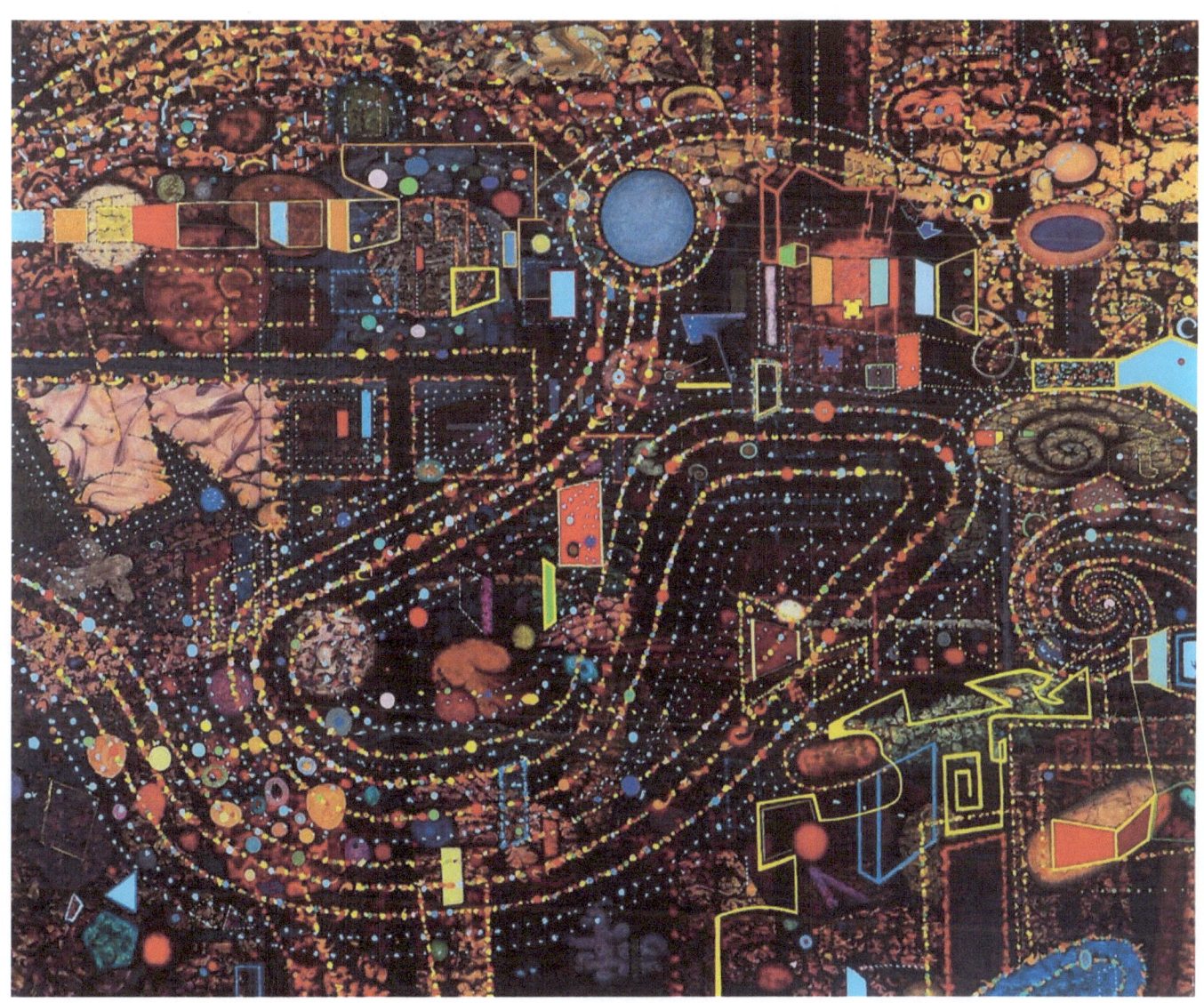

NODAL TRACES PASTORALE

2012 - 2014
Acrylic on Baltic Birch
24" x 24"

The organic quality of this work is palpable. It has an aliveness that speaks of fecund fields and growing things. It looks like a CT scan has been taken of a portion of the earth and we can see, deep within, the mechanics of the planet itself. Vytas makes us want to name and fix the elements in this painting but the beauty of this work is that we are not sure what any of it is. It seems we should know, and perhaps we did, before we reached the human stage of evolution. He reminds us of where we once were.

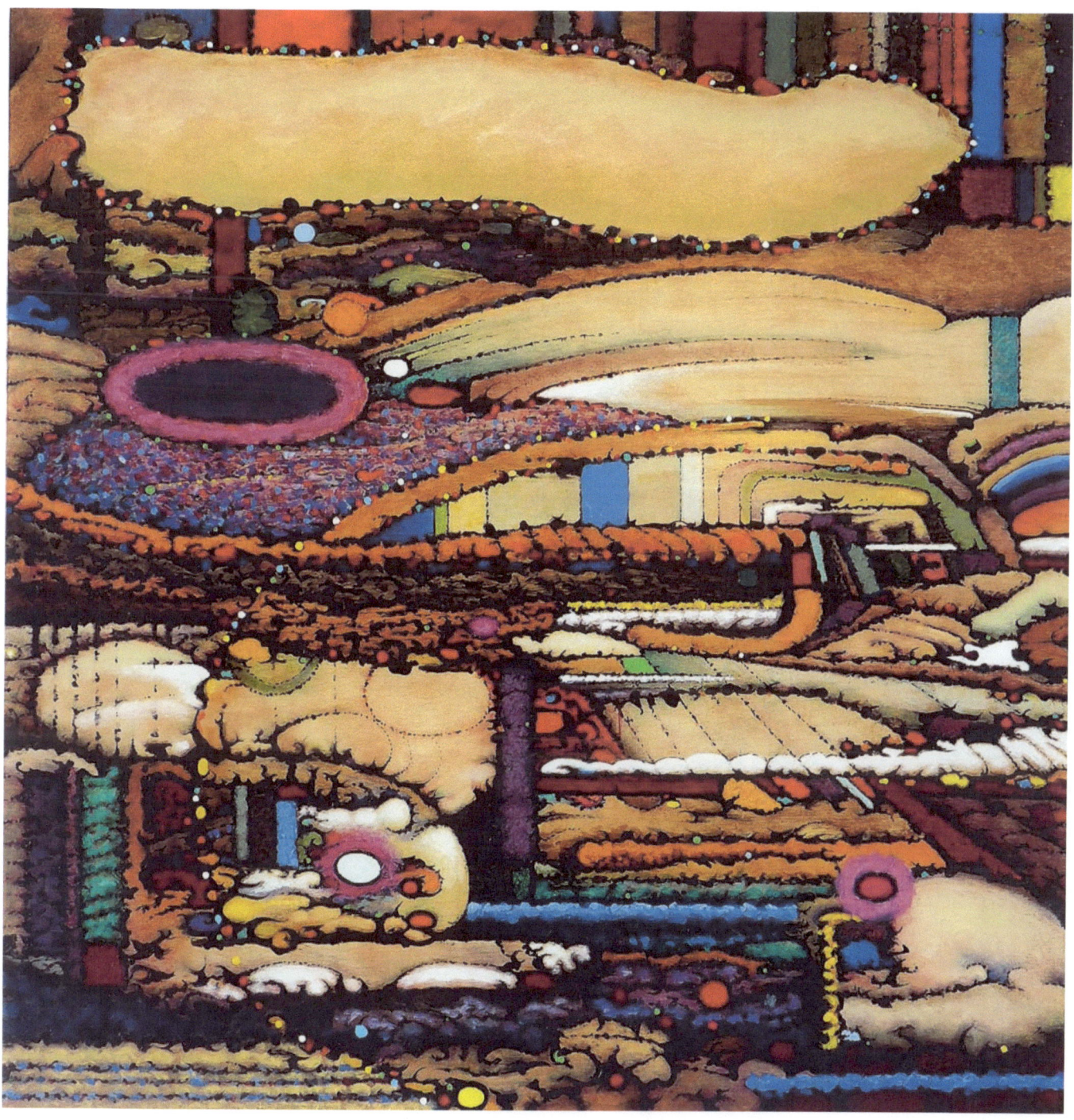

EYE WOULD 1

2012 - 2015
Acrylic on Baltic Birch
12" x 12"

This landscape is arid, barren yet seductive, evoking feelings of longing. Earth, dirt and sand have found their way into this scene. Vytas has brought them here with paint and brush creating a stopping place for us. Stock still we stand just outside this terrain and find the buried cache of turquoise, the beautiful object of our desire. That luscious glob of not-green, not-blue satisfies deeply.

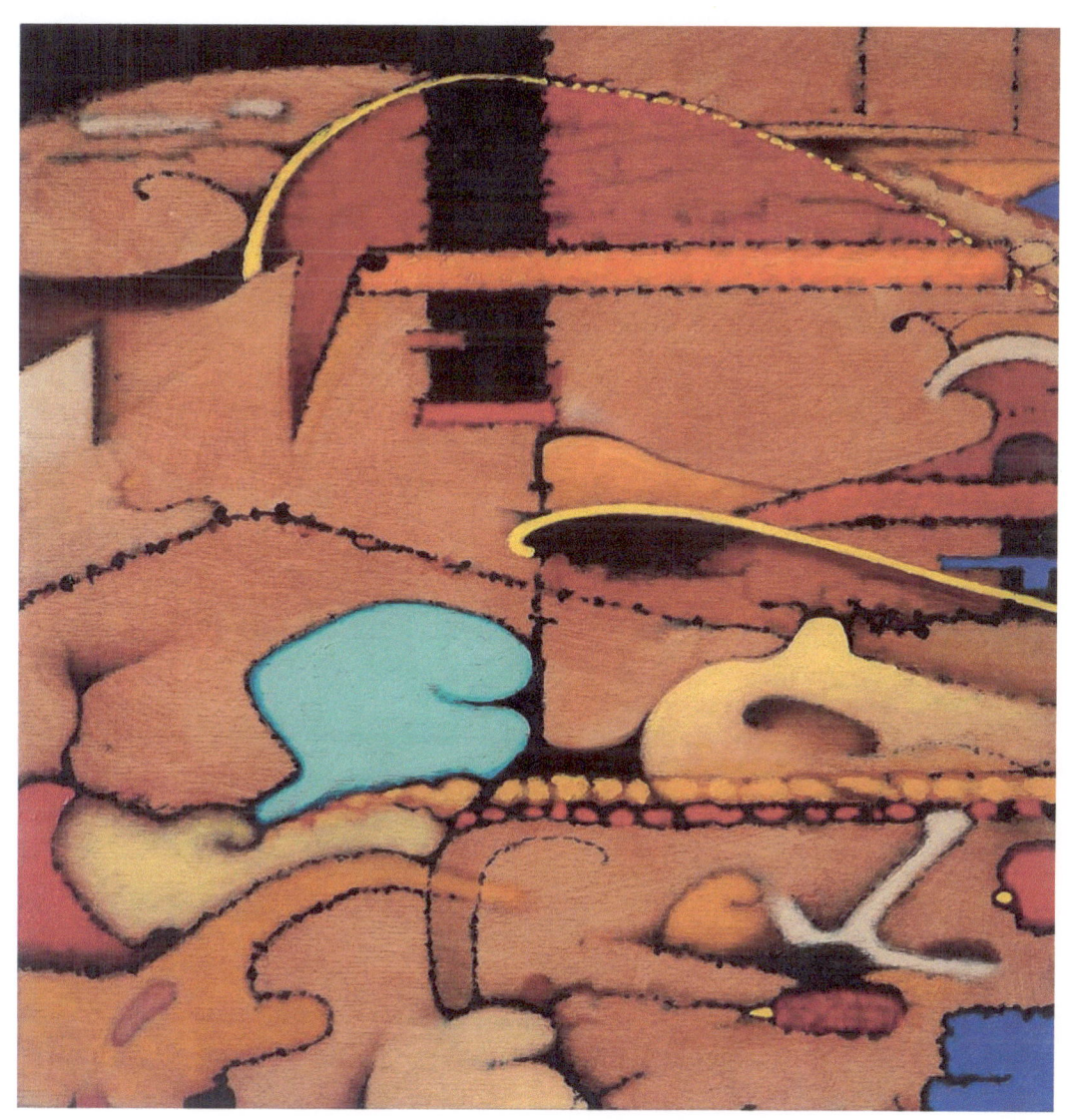

HOMAGE TO THE EARTH

2012 - 2014
Acrylic on Baltic Birch
12" x 12"

Deep within the heart of Gaia, that which will become mankind is suckling at the breast of nature. There is no part of what we become that is not indigenous. We are the product of fire, air, water and earth, with some star stuff thrown into the mix. There is great peace in this painting. It invites us into the womb of the world where we are safe and can dream of flying back into the stars.

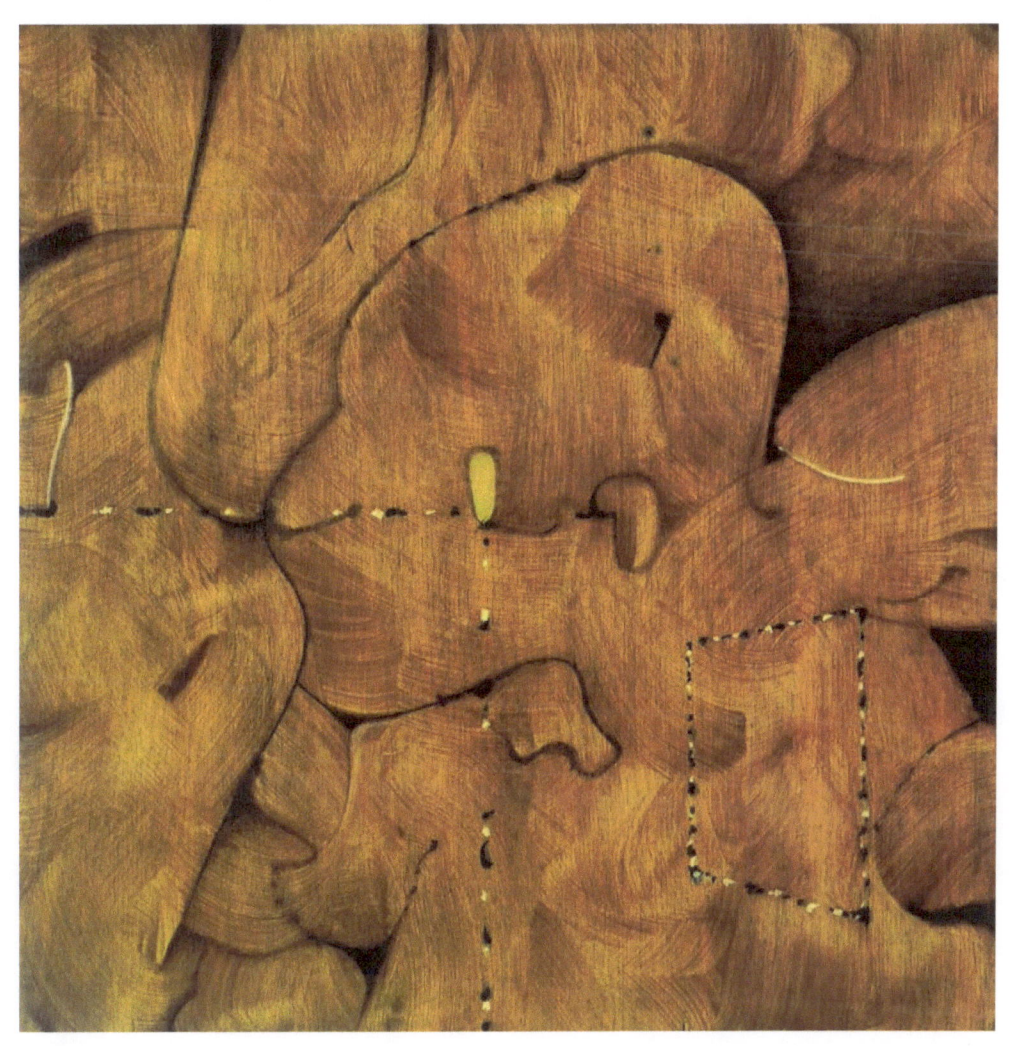

BLUE MATRIX

2012 - 2013
Acrylic on Canvas
60" x 48"

The shapes are entwined in great intricacy with lighter blue forms against a backdrop of darker blue. The curvilinear forms of this work imbue it with a soft, very accessible mood. There is a happy light-heartedness to this piece as if it might be depicting how our intestines would look after a great bout of laughter has moved through our entire being.

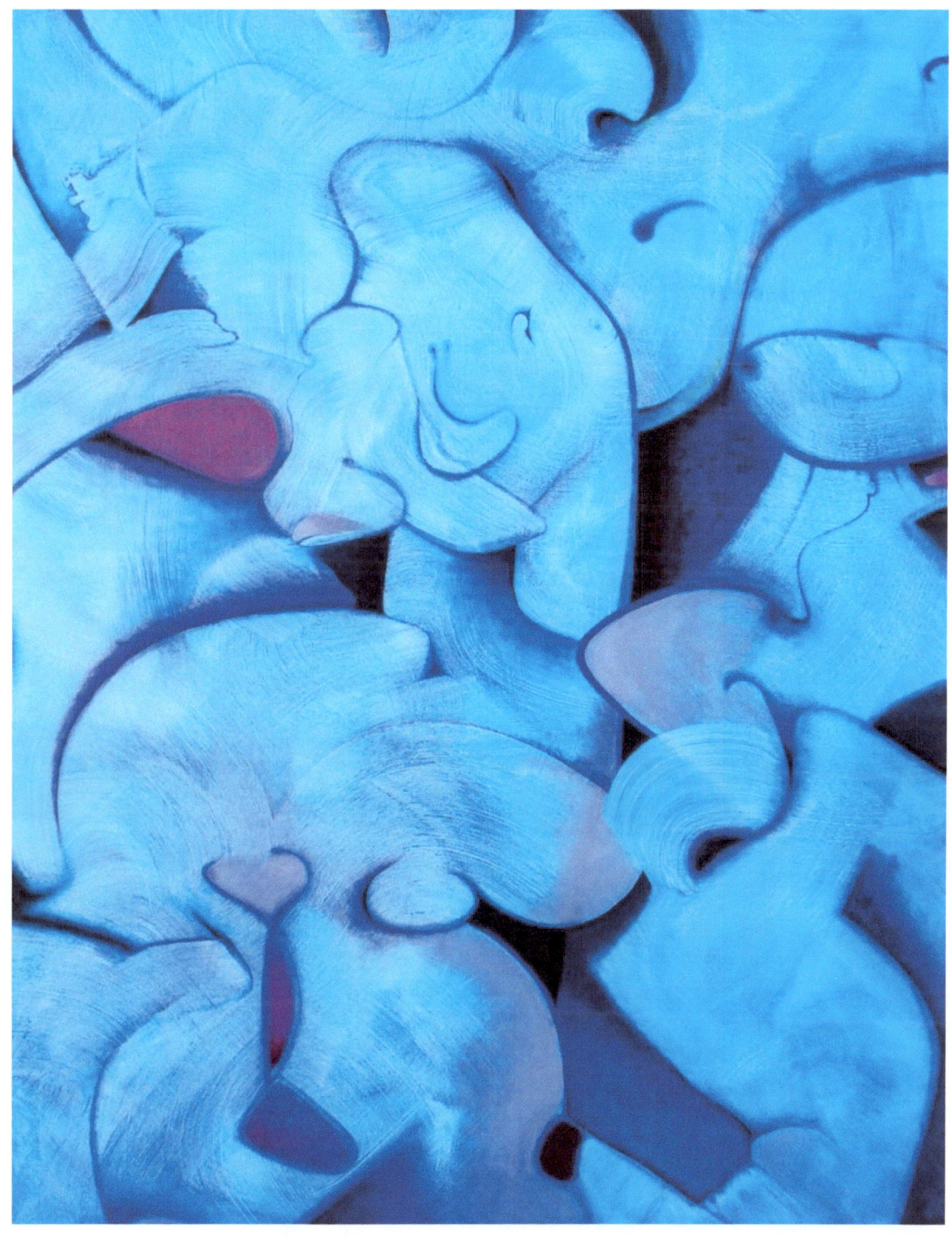

COSMIC VISTA

2012 - 2015
Acrylic on Canvas
36" x 48"

Time is the artist's gift to us. They spend hours plotting out the stream of moment-to-moment creation and leave their lives imprinted in the medium they have chosen. In this particular instance, Vytas gives us the impression that he has left a drop of his own life's blood upon the canvas. This cell, this drop of red, feeds the rest of the composition like a sun within a crowded sky. There is a space where the drop is penetrated so the life force within it can escape and touch us all.

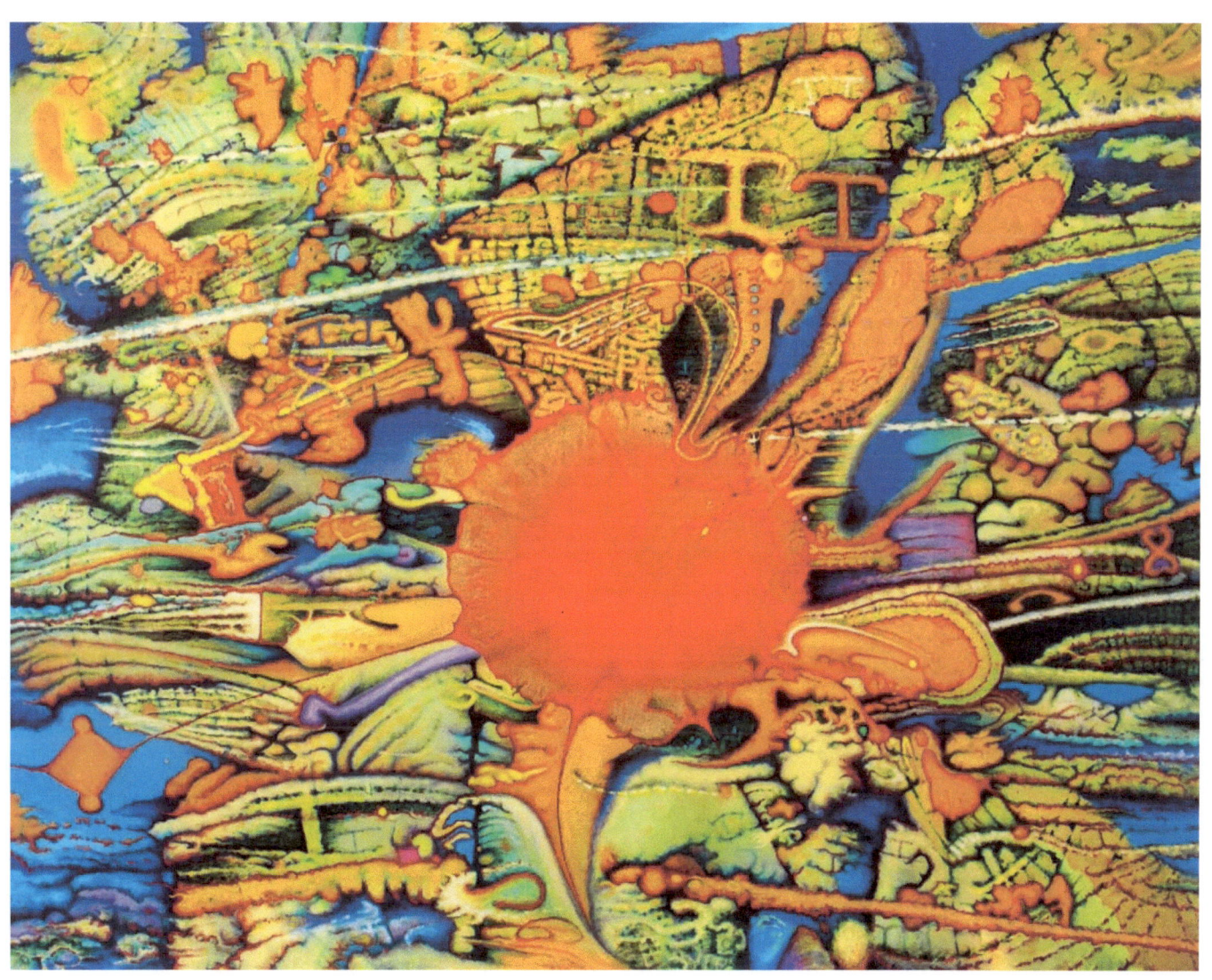

CHANCE BUDDHA

2012
Acrylic on Canvas
36" x 48"

This painting is the color of a lotus, so frequently associated with Buddha. Tender pink holds us in a warm embrace while we grapple with the freedom inherent in impermanence. Vytas captures a fragment of time and makes it permanent enough for us to have a glimpse of his vision. What is that part of us that believes we are not enlightened? That belief is an impediment to the realization of primordial wisdom; our Buddha Nature.

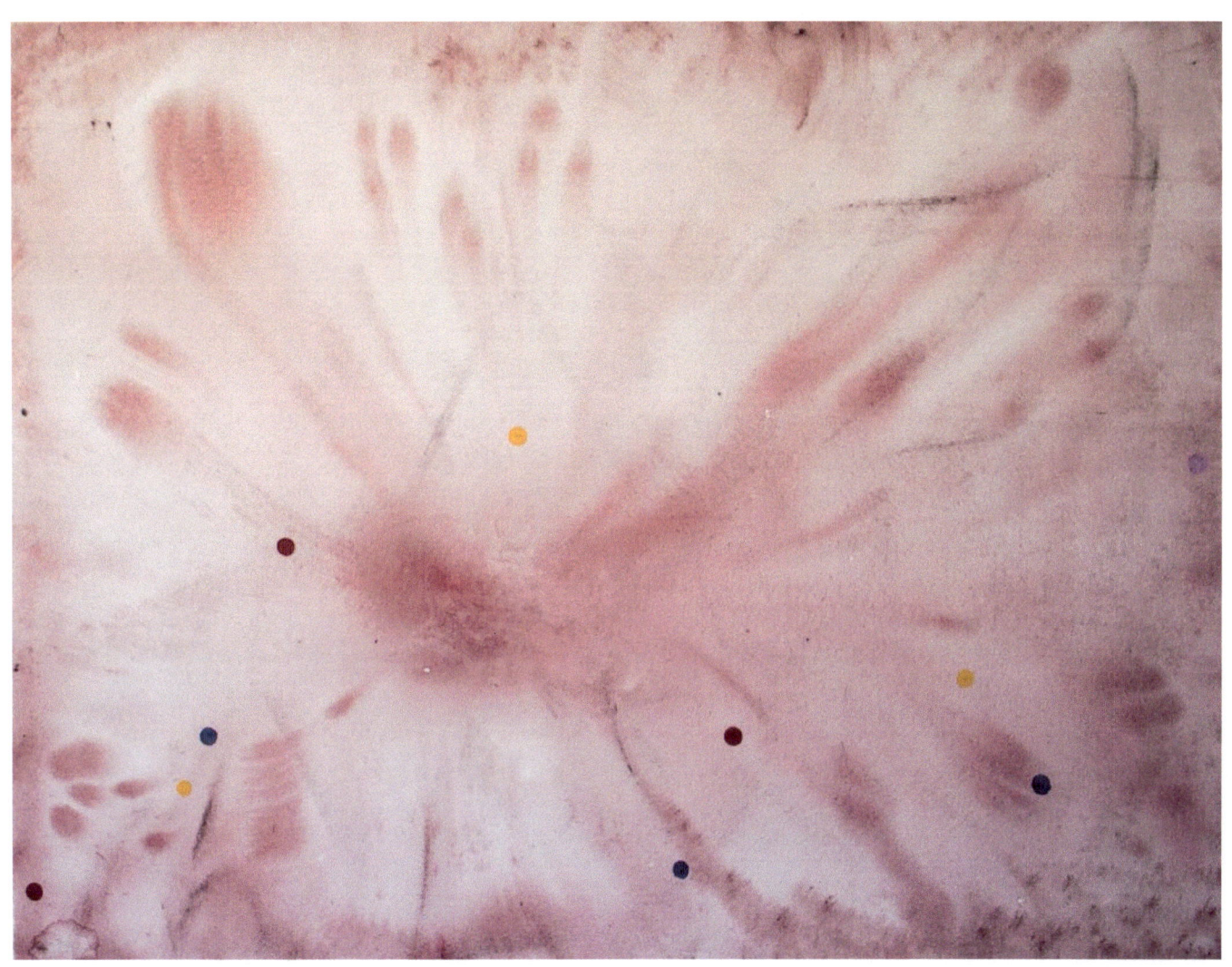

WRINKLE OF FANTASY 3

2013 - 2016
Acrylic on Wrinkled Canvas
73" x 58"

Vytas is representing the vital signs of the universe. He has scanned reality. His eye, acting like radar, has honed in on the pulsing rhythm of phenomena. Waves of vibrancy oscillate across the canvas and his brushwork looks as if he is painting with electricity. His is the uncanny ability to paint what is unseen, to uncover the obscured and make visible the fabric of the universe.

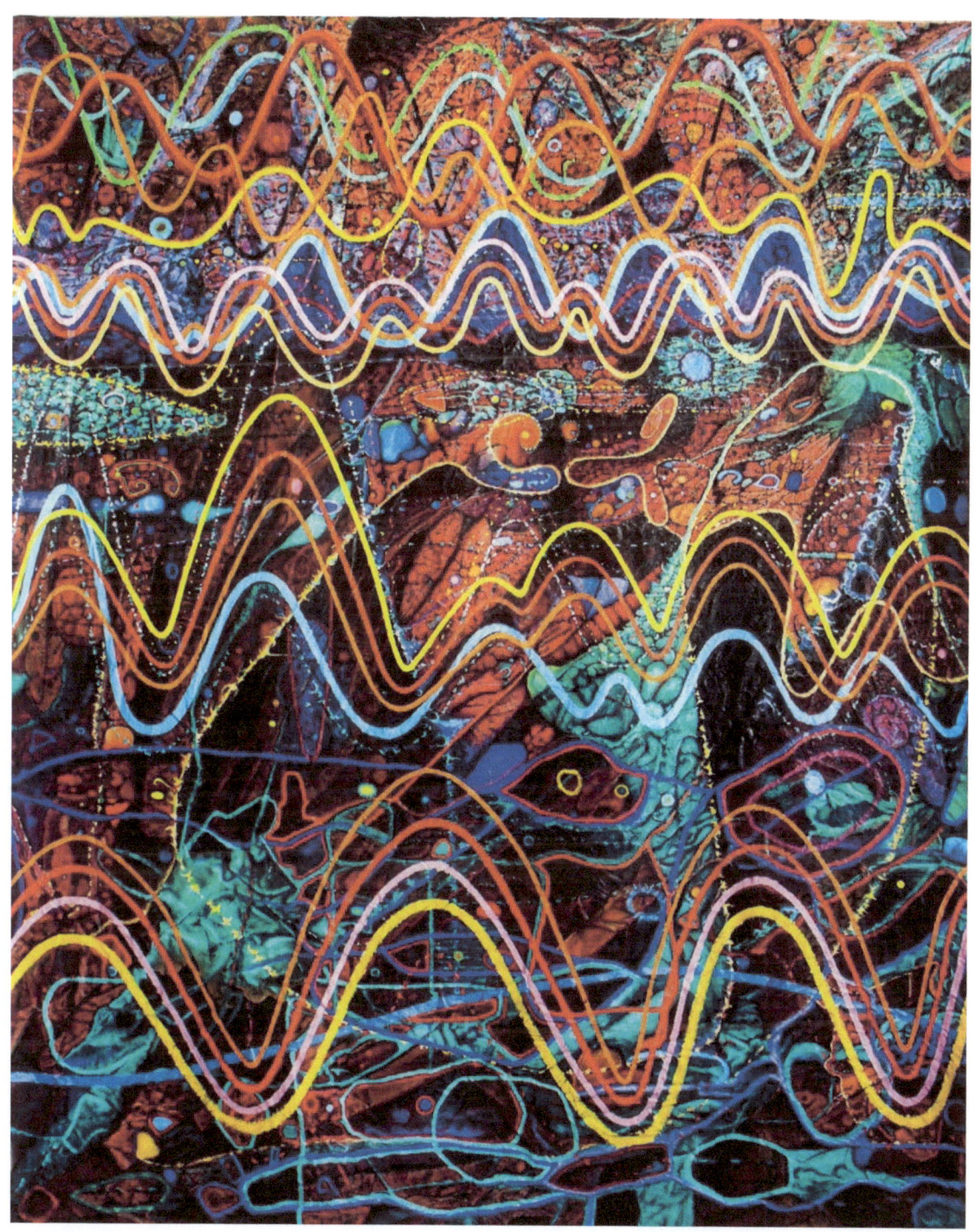

URBAN EYES

2014 - 2015
Acrylic on Canvas
28" x 22"

We all live here. We are confined within our own spaces separated by fences, individual houses, beliefs and customs. There are faint glimpses of green as though there is something vibrant and alive in some parts of a crowded cityscape. That something speaks to the part of us that wants to break down the boundaries, no matter how familiar and comfortable they are, and destroy the isolation. We want to find the persons inside those forms and invite them to join us in green parks. We want to play drums, hold hands and dance together.

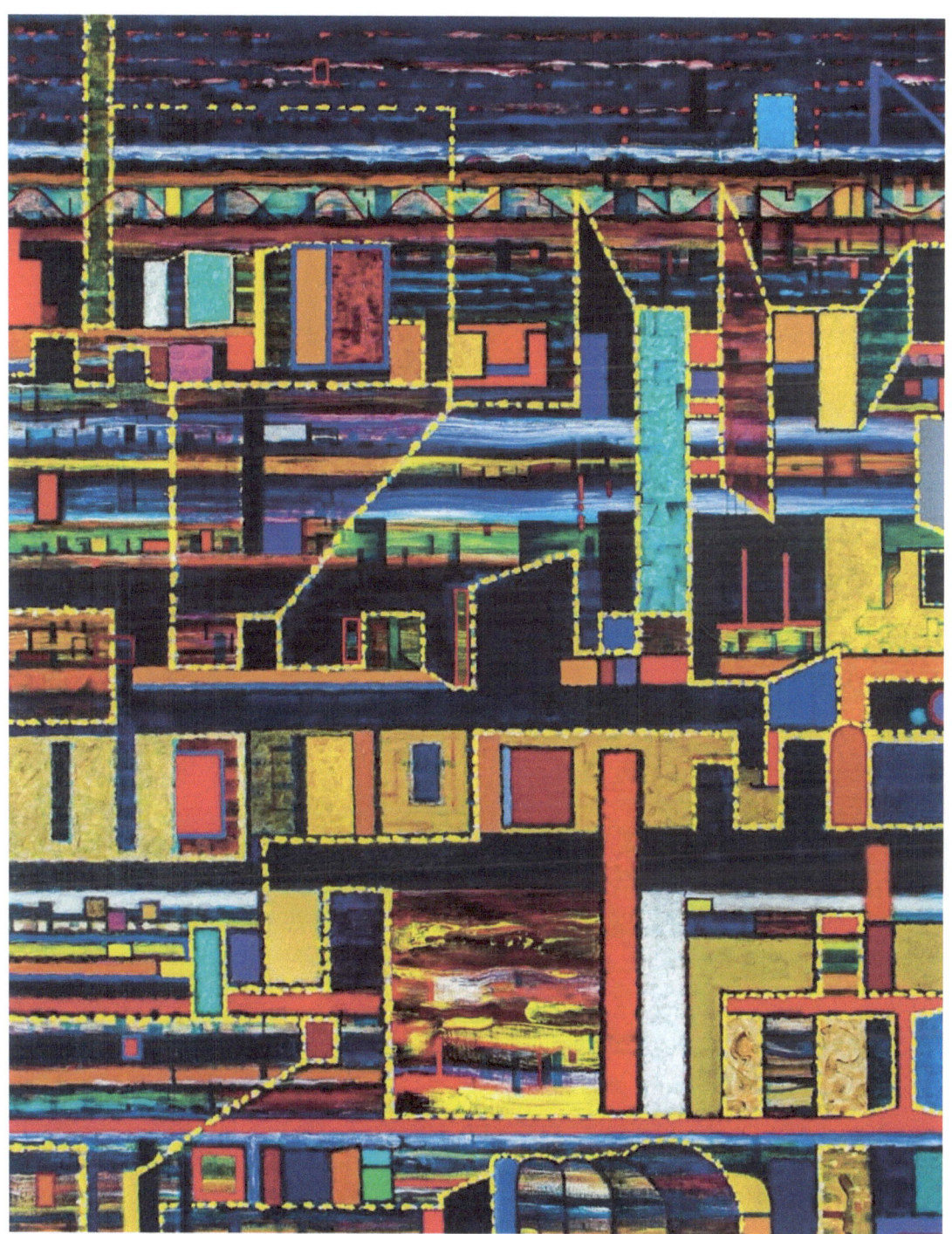

GOLDEN LIGHT

2006 - 2016
Oil on Canvas
30" x 24"

Yes, this is golden light. It is streaming, falling, forming and emanating in the vast darkness where it outlines fantastical shapes leading our minds and hearts into joyful play. It is the dance of Shiva, the wand of the Magus, the face of Maya. It reminds us that we are light beings looking into the twin mirrors of eternity and infinity: time and space.

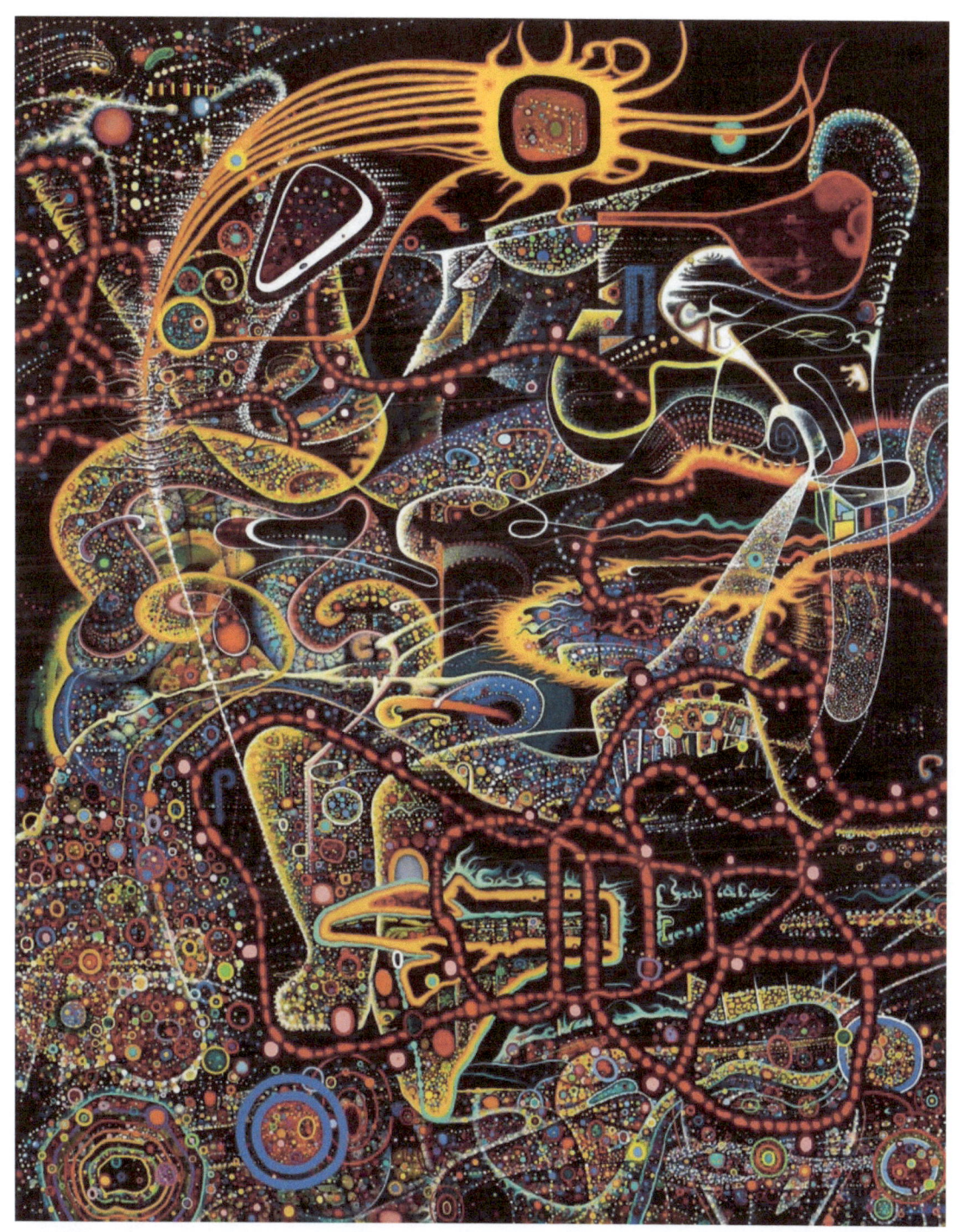

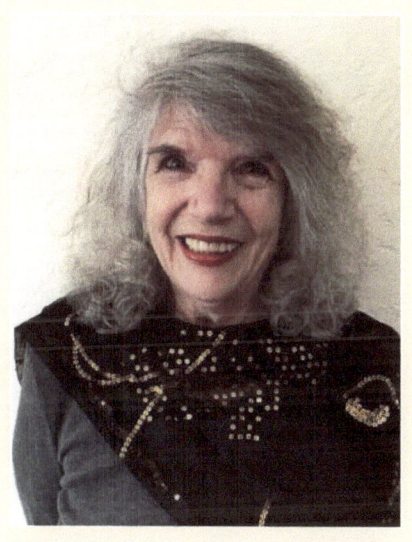

BONNIE BOSTROM, a writer and poet, as with this publication, works with talented people to produce books. Her first book, The Way-Showers, was a collaborative work with the sculptor, Joan Baliker. She then teamed with Barbara Reider, PhD., to write Women Facing Retirement: A Time for Self Reflection. Next, she published a collection of her poems entitled Quicksilver Dreams. She combined the love of writing and her aspirations as a student of Tibetan Buddhism to create, with photographer Bruce Shah, Buddha Nature of the Southwest.

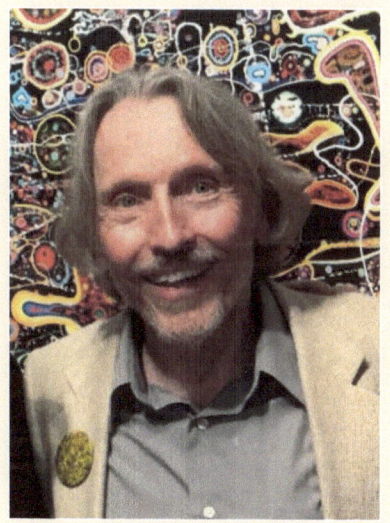

VYTAS SAKALAS (Vytautas Sakalauskas), an artist and drummer, was born in 1951, in Newark, New Jersey. His parents were Lithuanian immigrants. He studied at York College of the City University of New York, where he received a Bachelor of Arts in Fine Art in 1977. Before that, he attended Los Angeles City College where he received an Associate of Arts degree in Cinema in 1974. He currently resides in Tucson, Arizona.

www.sakalasart.com
sakalasart@gmail.com

A listing of his many exhibitions, collections, and other work follows.

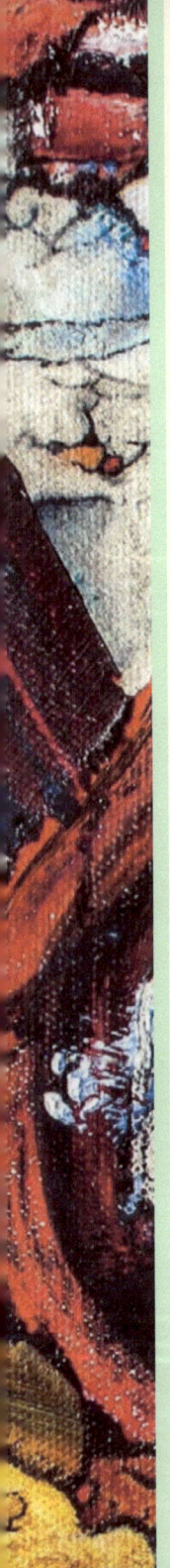

SELECTED SOLO EXHIBITIONS

2016 - Vytas Visions, Desert Art Museum, Tucson, AZ

2015 - Party Time, Home of Roger Weerasinghe, Tarzana, CA

2014 - Heal A Monster, University Medical Center South Campus, Tucson, AZ

2012/13 - 16 Paintings, Office of the Mayor, City of Tucson, AZ

2012 - In The Atmansphere, AI Gallery at Artisan Lofts, Phoenix, AZ

2010 - Doorway to Infinity, Contreras Gallery, Tucson, AZ

2008 - Together At Last, Art Institute of Tucson, Tucson, AZ

2008 - Desert Cubism, Grogan Gallery of Fine Art, Tucson, AZ

2006 - Ethereal Gravity, Grogan Gallery of Fine Art, Tucson, AZ

2006 - In Spring, Art Fare, Tucson, Arizona

2000 - Chthonic Djin, Imagine Art, Sedona, AZ

1999 - Between Calls, RAW Gallery, Tucson, AZ

1998 - Cowbizm and the Legend of Zeke and Clem, Temple of Music and Art, Tucson, AZ

1995 - Tranceformations: 25 Years of Work, University of Arizona Museum of Art, Tucson, AZ

1993 - New Paintings, Vartai Gallery, Vilnius, Lithuania

1993 - Mushroom Peace, Kaunas Picture Gallery, Kaunas, Lithuania

1993 - Prints and Drawings, Siauliai Art Gallery, Siauliai, Lithuania

1993 - Mushroom Peace, Center for Contemporary Art, Vilnius, Lithuania

1993 - Prints and Drawings, Kedainiai City Hall Gallery, Kedainiai, Lithuania

1993 - Prints and Drawings, Žilinskas Gallery, Kaunas, Lithuania

1991 - Vytas Sakalas: 20 Year Retrospective Exhibition, Lithuanian Museum of Art, Vilnius, Lithuania

1990 - Tentacle Foam, Lannon Gallery, Chicago, IL

1989 - Lines of Fate, Lannon Gallery, Chicago, IL

1989 - Lines of Fate, Arden Gallery, Boston, MA

1988 - An Esthetic Anesthetic, Gordon College, Essex, MA

1987 - Tranceformations, The Wet Gallery, Boston, MA

1986 - Recent Work: Paintings and Cutouts, Gallery on the Green, Lexington, MA

SELECTED GROUP EXHIBITIONS

2016 - Lithuanian Art Show, Hangar Gallery, Santa Monica, CA

2016 - 50th Anniversary Alumni Art Show, York College, C.U.N.Y., Jamaica, NY

2016 - Contempo: The New West, Four Corners Gallery, Tucson, AZ

2016 - The Horse Of Course, Four Corners Gallery, Tucson, AZ

2015 - Gallery Artists, Art All Ways, Los Angeles, CA

2015 – Harding Gallery, Brooklyn, New York

2014 - Fluxus, Liquid Art House, Boston, MA

2011 - Faculty Exhibition, Art Institute of Tucson

2011 - The Aesthetic Code: Unraveling the Secrets of Art, University of Arizona Museum of Art, Tucson, AZ

2010 - Faculty and Staff Exhibition, Art Institute of Tucson, Tucson, AZ

2009 - Seventeenth Spring Show, Jane Hamilton Fine Art, Tucson, AZ

2008 - Gallery Artists, Mountain Shadow Gallery, Tucson, AZ

2007 - Original Face, MicroCosm Gallery, New York, NY

2007 - Gallery Artists Show, Jessica Hagan Fine Art & Design, Newport, RI

2007 - Encircle, Grogan Gallery of Fine Art, Tucson, AZ

2007 - Imago, Grogan Gallery of Fine Art, Tucson, AZ

2006 - Uncommon, Platform Gallery, Tucson, AZ

2006 - Sex, Politics and Religion, Raices-Taller Gallery, Tucson, AZ

2005 - Out of Chaos, Liz Hernandez Gallery, Tucson, AZ

2005 - Holiday Bazaar, Museum of Contemporary Art, Tucson, AZ

2004 - Invitational, Raices-Taller Gallery, Tucson, AZ

2003 - Arizona Biennial Exhibition, Tucson Museum of Art, Tucson, AZ

2003 - 7 Thoughts, Lithuanian Museum of Art, Lemont, IL

2000 - For Pete's Sake, University of Arizona Museum of Art, Tucson, AZ

2000 - Yellow House Gallery, Fort Worth, TX

1999 - Yellow House Gallery, Fort Worth, TX

1998 - Tucson Artists: 1970-1997, Selections from the Permanent Collection, University of Arizona, Museum of Art, Tucson, AZ

1993 - Color, Texture, Detail, Arden Gallery, Boston, MA

1993 - Takada Fine Arts, San Francisco, CA

1993 - Congress Street Gallery, Tucson, AZ

1993 - Redstone Gallery, Sedona, AZ

1992 - Congress Street Gallery, Tucson, AZ

1992 - Redstone Gallery, Sedona, AZ

1990 - Elaine Horwitch Gallery, Sedona, AZ

1990 - Lee/Lanning Gallery, Sedona, AZ

1989 - Museum of Fine Arts, Boston, MA

1988 - Boston Drawing Show, Boston MA

1988 - Micro Phobia Macro Logia, Lannon Gallery, Chicago, IL

1988 - Inaugural Exhibit, Lannon Gallery, Chicago, IL

1988 - Boston Now: Works on Paper, Institute of Contemporary Art, Boston, MA

1987 - Triennial, Fuller Museum of Art, Brockton, MA

1987 - Illusion in Art: Perception/Description/Deception, Boston University Art Gallery, Boston, MA

1987 - Invitational, Stux Gallery, Boston, MA

1987 -Abstract Drawing, Westby Art Gallery, Glassboro State College, Glassboro, NJ

1986 - Selections 34, The Drawing Center, New York, NY

1986 - Design Studio A, Boston, MA

1977 - Razor Gallery, New York, NY

REVIEWS

Margaret Regan, Basics and Beyond, Tucson Weekly, Jan. 14-20 1999

Rayna Wagner, Airport Sculptures are Eye-catching and Functional, Arizona Daily Star, Oct. 30, 1996

Sarah R. Marino, Bilingualism in the Visual Arts, The Baltic Observer, Jan. 8-14, 1993

Charles Giuliano, Lines of Fate by Vytas Sakalas, Art New England, April, 1989

Christine Temin, The Paper Chase at the ICA, Boston Globe, July 24, 1988

Robin Hardman, Paper Chase, South End News, July 30, 1988

Charles Giuliano, Paper Trail, The Patriot Ledger, July 26, 1988

Mark Caro, Seeing is Disbelieving, The Boston Phoenix, Nov. 27 – Dec. 23, 1987

Robert Taylor, BU Show Offers More Than Meets the Eye, Boston Globe, Nov. 22, 1987

Carolyn Green, Vytas Sakalas: Beyond Post Modernism, Art New England, April, 1986

SELECTED COLLECTIONS

Museum of Fine Arts, Boston, MA

University of Arizona Museum of Art, Tucson, AZ

Busch-Reisinger Museum, Harvard University, Cambridge, MA

Boston Public Library, Boston, MA

Fuller Museum of Art, Brockton, MA

Lithuanian Museum of Art, Vilinius, Lithuania

National Ĉiurlionis Art Museum, Kaunas, Lithuania

Center for Contemporary Art, Vilnius, Lithuania

Šiauliai Art Gallery, Šiauliai, Lithuania

United States Embassy, Vilnius, Lithuania

Vilnius University, Vilnius, Lithuania

Vytautas Magnus University, Kaunas, Lithuania

The Process Museum, Tucson, AZ

Dorchester Courthouse Annex, Dorchester, MA

Brigham and Women's Hospital, Boston, MA

MetLife Insurance, Corporate Center, Marlborough, MA

Gillette Corporation, Boston, MA

Putnam Investments, Boston, MA

Lochridge and Company, Inc., Boston, MA

Coopers and Lybrand, Boston, MA

Cabot Company, Boston, MA

World Data Business, Kaunas, Lithuania

Nolan & Nolan, Inc., Lexington, MA

COMMISSIONS

The Boston Globe Newspaper Company, Boston, MA

One Mifflin Place, Cambridge, MA

Fidelity Investments, Boston, MA

Alcon Surgical, Irvine, CA

Lithuanian Bank of Commerce, Kaunas, Lithuania

Limited Editions, Philadelphia, Pennsylvania

DMR Group, Inc., Boston, MA

James and Shirley Koster, Tucson, AZ

PUBLIC ART COMMISSIONS

Silver Linings, acrylic on plasma-cut aluminum,
6' x 70', Tucson International Airport,
Tucson, AZ

TEACHING EXPERIENCE

2008-2013: Art Institute of Tucson,
Tucson, AZ

1992-1993: Vytautas Magnus University,
Kaunas, Lithuania

1992-1993: Lithuania Academy of Art,
Vilnius, Lithuania

1992-1993: Kaunas Art Institute,

Kaunas, Lithuania

COLLABORATIONS

1995-1996 with Edwards/Tanz Collaborative:
Tucson International Airport Concourse Divider

1993 -with Nijole Stunskaite: Castle Banner Series

1993 -with Algirdas Baranauskas, Ginutis Dudaitis,
Rimantas Gailiunus: Distaff Series

1993 -with Simas Miliunas, Architect:
Commissioned Diptych Painting

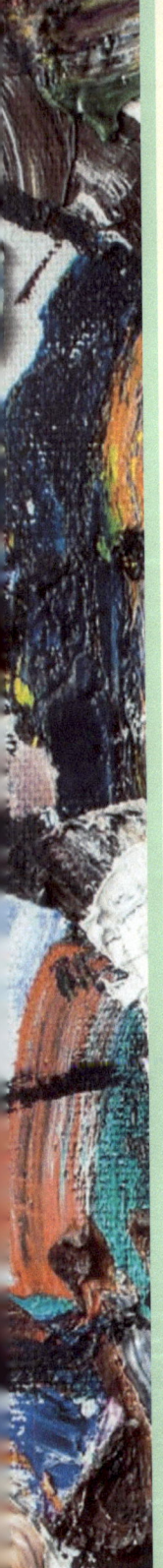

PERSPECTIVES

He'd been disappearing into my garage nearly every day for months. He was painting, that I knew. He had requested that I not view his work until he was ready, until I was invited. I honored this request, as I honored him. Out of the blue, this tall, angel-faced youth had shown up in my life.

Vytas had shown me some of his earlier drawings and paintings, which included many abstract and surrealist works, and a large 6' x 4' painting that Vytas had painted at age 12, a copy of a painting of Jesus praying in the Garden of Olives. In these early days (Vytas was only 18) I could see his talent. Even with this knowledge, nothing could have prepared me for what I beheld on the day he invited me to view "The Oneness." The canvas was large, 4' x 4'. It depicted various aspects of cosmic creation and evolution all merged into a harmonious whole around a central sun, earth core, or zygote. It was painted with attention to myriad details, from tiny organisms emerging from a primal sea, to forests, mountains, fungi, and nature spirits in a forming world. I stood, silent and thunderstruck, for minutes before I could speak.

Vytas was prolific and dedicated. His skills and sophistication as a painter grew exponentially over the next several years. His style transitioned to non-representational

with themes that were often profound.

I will never forget my first viewing of "The Noumenon." (The paradoxical title derives from Nietzsche's concept of an idea or object apprehended by the mind and not by the senses. Teilhard de Chardin's concept of the noosphere, a planet-enveloping field of life consciousness was also an idea that we had been discussing at the time). I was transfixed as the entire history of human art was inexplicably evoked by this single 30" x 24" oil painting propped against a wall of his little Echo Park apartment. Vytas had covered the entire history of art from cave painting through Egyptian glyphs, Medieval, Renaissance, and Impressionism, to Modern Art.

In 1974 Vytas left Los Angeles, where he had grown up, for New York City. He stayed in touch via letters, phone calls, and occasional visits. Years later, when he settled in Tucson, he set up a website. I had the occasion to visit his studio and view these works first hand.

His work is powerfully evocative, sparking in the viewer unexpected and amazing associations. In "Toward The Tortolitas" that stark mountain range looms in moonlight, in raging storms, in the dark of night, in summer heat and in winter snow, as life seethes and slithers in the writhing desert below, unearthing haunted caverns of buried civilizations. I marvel, "How….how am I seeing seasons, centuries, moments, eternities, captured here, now, all at once?"

There is something uncanny about Vytas' paintings. He reports going into a trance state while painting. Like a shaman, he delves into realms beyond the ordinary to tap into the primal morphogenic field, the womb of form, returning to entrance us with his art.

Dr. Julia Scofield Russell
Environmental Educator
Published in Eco-Home Network, Ecolution

I have known Vytas Sakalas for almost three years now. Although we are both essentially abstract painters, we use very different methods, processes, and seek to realize very different visions. However, I believe we bonded based on shared similar worldviews and a mutual desire to achieve something unique and personal in the work we produce. Also, it turned out, we are both serious musicians and both particularly involved in the aspects of rhythm. I have seen a fair amount of Vytas' older work and while seeing bits of influence from different stylistic schools, especially cubism I could see, emerging over time, a very specific individual vision and realization.

I think the most important point is the singularity of achievement in the quest for his unique vision. I once told a musician friend of mine that he should not suffer to be told he was "gifted" when what he was, in fact, was extraordinarily accomplished. The same applies in Vytas' case. The "gift" he received is one of a passion that has driven him to work for the patience, tenacity, and unwavering dedication absolutely required in manifesting a distinctive and personal vision. In doing so, he has achieved that rarest of accomplishments. He has created a body of work that defies any categorization, brooks no comparison, and is completely original on its own.

Greg Chandler, Artist/Musician
www.gregorypchandler.com

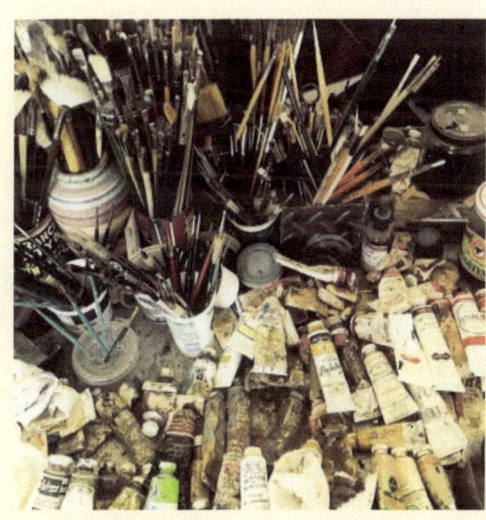

ACKNOWLEDGMENTS

Special thanks to Cynthia Childers for introducing me to Vytas Sakalas and to Vytas for introducing me to his world. The following people helped make it possible to introduce Vytas' world to you. I am grateful for their support, encouragement and enthusiasm. Thanks dear friends.

Abhishiktananda

Arūnas Baltėnas

Orit Bornstein

Jim Bostrom

Greg Chandler

Haley Fryling

Wilson Graham

Greg Hart

Pat Hills

Juanita Cheng-McCarron

Linda Petersen

Julia Russell

Paulo Lima Santos

John Saunders

Athena Steen

Bill Steen

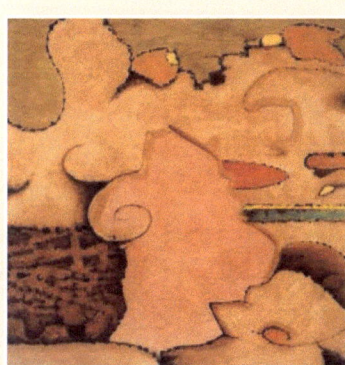

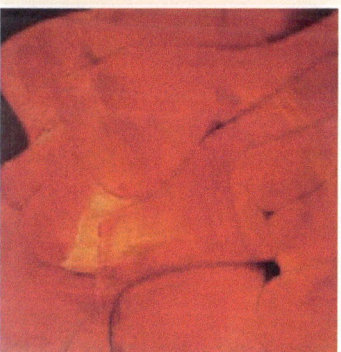

Copyright 2017
Bonnie Bostrom
ISBN 978-099862780

Vytas Sakalas retains
all rights to his images

Published by
the Canelo Project
www.caneloproject.com
caneloproject@gmail.com

Layout and Design by
Athena Swentzell Steen

Photographs by
John Saunders
Bill Steen
Wilson Graham
Arūnas Baltėnas
Vytas Sakalas

Edited by
Linda Petersen

www.ingramcontent.com/pod-product-compliance
Lightning Source LLC
Chambersburg PA
CBHW050848180526
45159CB00007B/2613